River Tyne Trail: sources to sea

The Daft as a Brush
Cancer Patient Care Walk

Peter Donaghy & John Laidler

SIGMA Leisure

Published by Sigma Leisure – an imprint of Sigma Press, Stobart House, Pontyclerc, Penybanc Road, Ammanford, Carmarthenshire SA18 3HP.

British Library Cataloguing in Publication Data
A CIP record for this book is available from the British Library.

ISBN: 978-1-910758-02-1

Typesetting and Design by: Sigma Press, Ammanford.

Cover photographs: © Graeme Peacock

Photographs: © Peter Donaghy unless stated otherwise.

Drawn maps: © Sigma Press

Inside cover outline map: © Dave Harrison

Mapping data Licenced from Ordnance Survey © Crown Copyright 2015 FL-GV100032058

Printed by: Akcent Media Limited

Some thoughts from Brian Burnie, founder of the Cancer Charity, Daft as a Brush Cancer Patient Care

Thank you for buying this book on the walk and in so doing, contributing to the charity. I trust it helps you to enjoy a rather special and unique walk through some of Great Britain's most beautiful countryside.

In March 2012 I was part of the original pilot walk from the source of the South Tyne at Geoff and Barbara Carrick's farm and the North Tyne at Jimmy and Fiona Hall's farm, with three Daft as a Brush volunteers, Dave Bowmaker, Ron Stanley and an old friend of some 50 years, Bill King "Red Socks" who travelled up from Cambridgeshire. At that time Bill had had cancer twice - kidney and prostate. Obviously we were all overjoyed when we eventually reached the pier at South Shields, no more than Bill who hugged us all and said that he was determined not to let cancer beat him in completing the 135-mile walk - now there is a challenge for everyone doing the walk!

Later I was introduced to Peter Donaghy and John Laidler who had previously produced a number of walking books. I asked if they would be interested in writing this book - a walk that is dedicated to all those people who have been affected by cancer. Within about five minutes, whilst I bribed them with a Greggs' bacon sandwich and a Wagon Wheel biscuit, they kindly agreed. However, there was one stipulation - they wanted all the proceeds of the sale of the book to go to Daft as a Brush Cancer Patient Care. Albeit, too many to mention, but this truly extraordinary walk would not have been possible without the help and assistance of all those very special people and organisations who have been involved in its creation - many, many thanks.

Hopefully, the walk will raise an awareness nationally of the difficulties cancer patients face on a daily basis getting to and from hospital whilst having treatment for cancer. Regionally the charity, Daft as a Brush Cancer Patient Care, transports outpatients, free of charge, from the three northern counties to the Northern Centre for Cancer Care at the Freeman Hospital for their radiotherapy and/or chemotherapy treatment. The charity has a fleet of 18 ambulances; all staffed with a crew of two - a chauffeur

Brian with Daft as a Brush Cancer Patient Care ambulances

because they drive VIPs (Very Important Patients) together with a companion to assist the patient and to make their journey comfortable and stress free. This service is only made possible by the dedication of a magnificent team of some 200 volunteers. The high quality service they provide to patients is what they would like to receive if they were in a similar position. Coming from a business background, I have always said you could not pay people to work as hard as the volunteers do 'for free'. Thank you to all the staff at

Daft as a Brush and at The Northern Centre for Cancer Care for making this outstanding work possible.

To the future - hopefully, through this walk, there will be a greater understanding of the work of the charity and, with the help and assistance of people from across Great Britain, the service that is provided to cancer patients in the North of England may become available nationally and, who knows, even internationally.

People might like to do the walk, or sections of it, to raise money for cancer research or Daft as a Brush Cancer Patient Care and/or in memory of a loved one, or simply for the pleasure of the route. However, don't forget, when you reach either Tynemouth or South Shields pier to give it a kiss or give your friends a hug - just as 'Red Socks' did - very well done!

Brian Burnie

Some key players welcome the arrival of the stone obelisk
From left to right: William King, Brian Burnie, Dave Bowmaker, Gilbert Ward (Stone Sculptor), Ron Stanley, Robert Charlton (the owner of Border Stone Quarry who kindly donated the stone)

(*Photograph: Steve Watson*)

DAFT AS A BRUSH

Well, it is all said in the title; but what lies behind Brian Burnie and his vision to help cancer patients?

Brian is a successful businessman and philanthropist, born in the north east and always willing to provide support for worthy causes. A few years ago he recognised the exceptional needs of patients receiving cancer care, especially those who had to travel long distances on a daily basis for radiotherapy treatment. The ambulance service would pick them up early in the morning, call for other patients on the way and return them home in the early evening ready to start again the next morning. Not surprising that patients describe this as the worst part of a nightmare cancer journey.

Brian had the idea to provide a bespoke service staffed by volunteers: an individual service in a comfortable vehicle, shortening travel time by up to 80%, home for morning coffee and the rest of the day to recover. No wonder that some of the patients said that without the service they would have given up. Brian sold his country house hotel at Doxford and set up the Daft as a Brush charity. Here is not the place to debate the origins of the phrase "Daft as a Brush", suffice to say it is a term of endearment, implying a slightly eccentric but loveable character that accurately reflects both Brian and some of his apparently crazy ideas.

The walk itself is another brainchild of Brian and does indeed reflect the cancer patient's journey. From the wilderness of diagnosis and the sources of the mighty river to a new dawn as the sun rises over the sea. Along the way there are 82 river crossings which perhaps represent the hurdles along the cancer journey.

We know that you will enjoy the walk, but along the way just give some thought to those on a different long distance journey.

Sir Alan Craft
Emeritus Professor
of Child Health
Trustee of Daft as a Brush Cancer
Patient Care

CONTENTS

To all those people who have been affected by cancer

Sir Leonard Fenwick CBE, Chief Executive of the Newcastle upon Tyne Hospitals NHS Foundation Trust with Brian Burnie, Trustee of the charity Daft as a Brush Cancer Patient Care. Pictured are volunteers and ambulances that transport, free of change, patients for treatment at hospital.

(*Photograph: Tony Iley*)

FOREWORD by STING

I was born and raised no more than a stone's throw from the banks of the River Tyne. Not that you could ever see the river from our house in Gerald Street because for most of the year the view would be blocked by the massive bow of a ship under construction at the Swan Hunter Shipyard in Wallsend.

I've seen bigger rivers in my time, of course, but there is something special about my river, the river that spawned me. Throughout my childhood I would make this pilgrimage whenever I could, to stand and watch and marvel at what seemed, at the time, a vast body of moving water, a living thing, a silent and ancient spirit, albeit dirty and awash with the detritus of the industry along its banks but nevertheless strong and sinuous, flowing continuously for millennia, century after century. And I would imagine how many dreamers like me would have walked down its shores and wondered at its mysteries. Ancient Britons, Celts, Picts, Roman centurions, Saxons, Christian saints and scholars, industrialists, inventors, poets and the odd singer, all recognised this same river, this symbol of continuity, of commerce and spirit.

It is in this spirit of pilgrimage that Peter Donaghy and John Laidler have compiled their guidebook; a walk alongside the Tyne from its twin sources in the Cheviots and the Pennines and following its storied banks all the way to the North Sea. Like all good pilgrims, they have honoured the river's rich and varied history, its vitality, its topography, its twists and turns, its surprises. It is also entirely appropriate that the guidebook is presented in tandem with the charity, Daft as a Brush Cancer Patient Care, what better symbol for healing than the irrepressible Tyne, where salmon now return to spawn, and its persistent flow of grace through the land of the Geordies.

I wish them all the best with this book and look forward to putting on 'me ould wahkin byuts' and joining them for another pilgrimage along our own sacred river.

GAN Canny!

Sting

INTRODUCTION

The idea, for a 135-mile long-distance walk from the sources of the Tyne to where the river reaches the sea, was the brainchild of Brian Burnie. Former businessman Brian is the founder of the charity, Daft as a Brush Cancer Patient Care. He believes that such a walk may have particular relevance for people affected, in one way or another, by cancer. Brian and Sir Alan Craft have provided some details of the Daft as a Brush story on the previous pages.

Brian recognised the wonderful variety of terrain and scenery that would be experienced on such a walk: hills and dales, sparsely populated landscapes, the largest man-made lake in Northern Europe, gentle pastures of arable and livestock farming, Roman remains, other historical and cultural connotations, the regeneration of former industrial areas and the changing moods of the river. He believed that completion of even part of the trail would be extremely gratifying for the walker. Moreover, its existence would generate interest in, and publicity for, the charity, particularly if a walkers' guide was available. After seeing a review of one of our earlier books, *Discovering Newcastle Gateshead*, Brian approached us to see if we would prepare the guidebook. It did not take long for Brian's canny persuasions to convince us that we should agree to his request.

There were only two criteria that Brian asked us to take into account in preparing this walk; first, where possible the walk should be alongside the river; second, reference should be made to the number of existing river crossings – it comes as a surprise to most people that there are some eighty-two crossings in all. With regard to walking near the river, in the main the trail does run alongside the river. However, currently, there are places where there are no available footpaths close to the river, either because the land there is privately owned and there is no public right of way, or because local conditions, for example erosion, make the riverbank unsuitable for walking. As the trail follows public and permissive rights of way, it is generally well waymarked with fingerposts and yellow arrows, some of which are on existing routes, for example, on parts of the South Tyne Trail and Hadrian's Wall Path.

Where the walk moves away from the riverside, it usually continues along public footpaths but there is a limited amount of road walking. This obviously requires the walker to take greater care. In most cases the trail follows fairly quiet minor roads but inevitably, on a few occasions, we need to use short sections of busier roads. Due care and attention also needs to be paid on those sections of the trail which are shared with cyclists. We have met Brian's second criterion by indicating, in the instructions for each stage, the number of river crossings there are in that particular stretch of river - even though not every crossing is encountered on the walk.

There are three sections in the walk corresponding to the three rivers that constitute the Tyne. The sources of the River Tyne are both located in fairly remote areas: the North Tyne at Deadwater in the Cheviot Hills, very close to the English-Scottish border and just north of Kielder in Northumberland; the South Tyne in the Pennine Hills near Garrigill beyond Alston in Cumbria. The two rivers converge at Warden, west of Hexham in Northumberland, from where the River Tyne makes its way to the sea. At the mouth of the river there are two towns; on the north bank is the aptly-named Tynemouth while South Shields occupies a similar position on the river's south side. The walker can choose to finish at either.

The walk is divided into twelve convenient stages based on ease of access and availability of transport and accommodation. Furthermore there are additional entry and exit points within each stage as appropriate. The stages do not necessarily represent daily sections, although the long-distance walker could use these as the basis to complete the walk; rather the aim is to provide an opportunity for the walker to follow the three components of the Tyne either as a continuum or on a piecemeal basis. In other words, this enables both long-distance walkers and day-walkers to create their own itinerary according to their ability and the time available.

For each stage we have made reference to the relevant Ordnance Survey (OS) maps which should be carried, refreshment possibilities and, to assist with the planning of individual itineraries, various entry and exit points.

Reference to the availability of refreshments does not necessarily imply recommendations and opening hours as well as other venues should be researched on the internet where possible. Outline maps show the entire route for each stage, for quick reference, and as a guide to both the entry and exit points. There is an introduction to each stage which provides information about the terrain and, for example, the amount of road walking. This is followed by detailed directions for the route together with relevant sections of the appropriate OS map (1:25 000 scale). In order to facilitate ease of access for walkers to the detailed route-directions, historical and cultural references have generally been kept in separate vignettes. You are advised to read through the information for each stage before deciding whether or not to embark upon it or at what point to join or leave it. The distances are as near to reality as possible but conditions, diversions and sightseeing may make for slight variations.

Occasionally, we have made a subjective choice between possible alternative routes. For example, you can walk from Kielder Village to the Kielder Dam using either the north shore or the south shore paths. On both paths, mobile reception is at best, intermittent. An added disadvantage on the north shore is that the walker has no exit points from the eleven mile stretch, whereas there are several exit possibilities along the south shore. Hence, our choice was to use the south shore path in Stage 1. For the section of the River Tyne east from Hexham to NewcastleGateshead there are several possibilities for walks on both sides of the river. We explored all of these before reaching our decision as to which are the most appropriate to incorporate into the long-distance walk. On four occasions we have provided optional shorter or easier routes alongside roads which might be of benefit to those wishing to cover longer distances in limited time. For the final stage of the river's journey to the sea, particularly for day-walkers, we have provided a choice of routes to either Tynemouth or South Shields.

You can, of course, expect seasonal variations. Little-used footpaths can become overgrown in summer and riverside and woodland paths extremely muddy in winter. When walking on roads, due care must be taken and some form of high-visibility clothing is advisable. The basic rule is to walk on the side which faces the oncoming traffic but, on some of the zig-zag sections on narrow minor roads occasional, judicious use of the other side might be advantageous. We have tried to ensure that the directions and other information are correct. However, it is inevitable that changes will occur – for example, signs fall into disrepair, gates and stiles are replaced, paths are diverted, trees are felled and even metal plaques and benches disappear!

It is our hope that this guidebook will not only help to create greater awareness of the charity but that it will also help to raise funds for the charity itself, for example, through encouraging sponsored walks. As the writers of this book we are delighted that all royalties on its sale will be paid directly to Daft as a Brush Cancer Patient Care.

In preparing this guidebook we have thoroughly enjoyed discovering more about our region and we just hope that you too will derive pleasure from the Daft as a Brush Cancer Patient Care Walk.

Finally, a word about respect. Do be careful to respect yourself by ensuring that you only attempt what you are physically capable of achieving, that you are properly clothed, including appropriate footwear and you are equipped for the conditions you might encounter. Please always respect the environment in which you are walking by following the country code.

Peter Donaghy and John Laidler

ACKNOWLEDGEMENTS

We are grateful for the assistance we have received from a great number of people. However, it would be impossible to name all those involved, be they staff from the various local authorities through which the Tyne flows, staff from Northumbria Water, Kielder Water and Development Trust, Tourist Information Centres, or well-informed private individuals.

Nevertheless, first and foremost, we must thank Brian Burnie for inviting us to prepare this guidebook and his hands-on and boots-on contributions. Indeed it was Brian and his friends Bill King, Ron Stanley and Dave Bowmaker whose pilot walk in 2012 provided the template for this book. Furthermore, Brian's wish for the walk to raise awareness of Daft as a Brush Cancer Patient Care, led, in October 2013, to the erection of the giant stone obelisk, provided by quarry owner Robert Charlton and sculptured by Gilbert Ward, that marks the source of the North Tyne. Here we must recognise the importance of the cooperation of Jimmy and Fiona Hall on whose land at Deadwater Farm the stone now stands and the walk commences. We would also like to express our thanks to Andrew Douglas for access across his land to the Border Counties Railway.

Jimmy and Fiona Hall,
Deadwater Farm
(Photograph: Eddie Carson)

Geoff and Barbara Carrick,
High Crossgill Farm
(Photograph: Eddie Carson)

Likewise we have enjoyed the support of Geoff and Barbara Carrick at High Crossgill Farm through whose land the South Tyne begins its journey. In addition we are grateful to English Heritage at Tynemouth and South Tyneside Council at South Shields for their permission to erect marker stones indicating the official ends of the walk. In regard to these two stones, once again we appreciate the contribution of Robert Charlton and Gilbert Ward. We are indebted to Tim Fish Northumberland County Council Footpaths Officer for his help in clarifying rights of way and potential problem sections. We are delighted with the help given by Professor Sir Alan Craft and thank him for highlighting the role of Brian Burnie in establishing Daft as a Brush Cancer Patient Care.

A great number of sources of information were used in researching the walk but we must single out three invaluable publications, namely Ron Thornton's beautifully illustrated *The River Tyne from sea to source* (Zymurgy Publishing, 2002) and J B Jonas's two helpful collections of walks, *Walking the Tyne* (Ramblers' Association, 3rd revised edition 2004) and *Walking the North Tyne* (Ramblers' Association, 2005).

We are grateful to family and friends who have checked various parts of the walk. However, in particular we must thank, Richard and Pat Page and Jeanne Donaghy who have not only walked the Trail as it stands but who have also explored the many alternative routes available. Their constructive criticism has greatly helped to shape the final outcome. We also wish to acknowledge the part played by the late Gillian Laidler in our previous books – a source of inspiration for us to continue walking and writing.

Finally, we would like to express our gratitude to Mike Newton for his patient proof-reading; to staff and volunteers at Daft as a Brush, especially to Jean Ross and Anne Pitkethly; to Dave Harrison for his important design and website contributions; to Graeme Peacock for his photographs as acknowledged throughout the text; and, of course, to Jane Evans, Steve Cooper and all at Sigma Leisure for their guidance and invaluable help in bringing this book to fruition. While any errors or omissions are solely our responsibility, any corrections can be forwarded to us through Sigma Leisure.

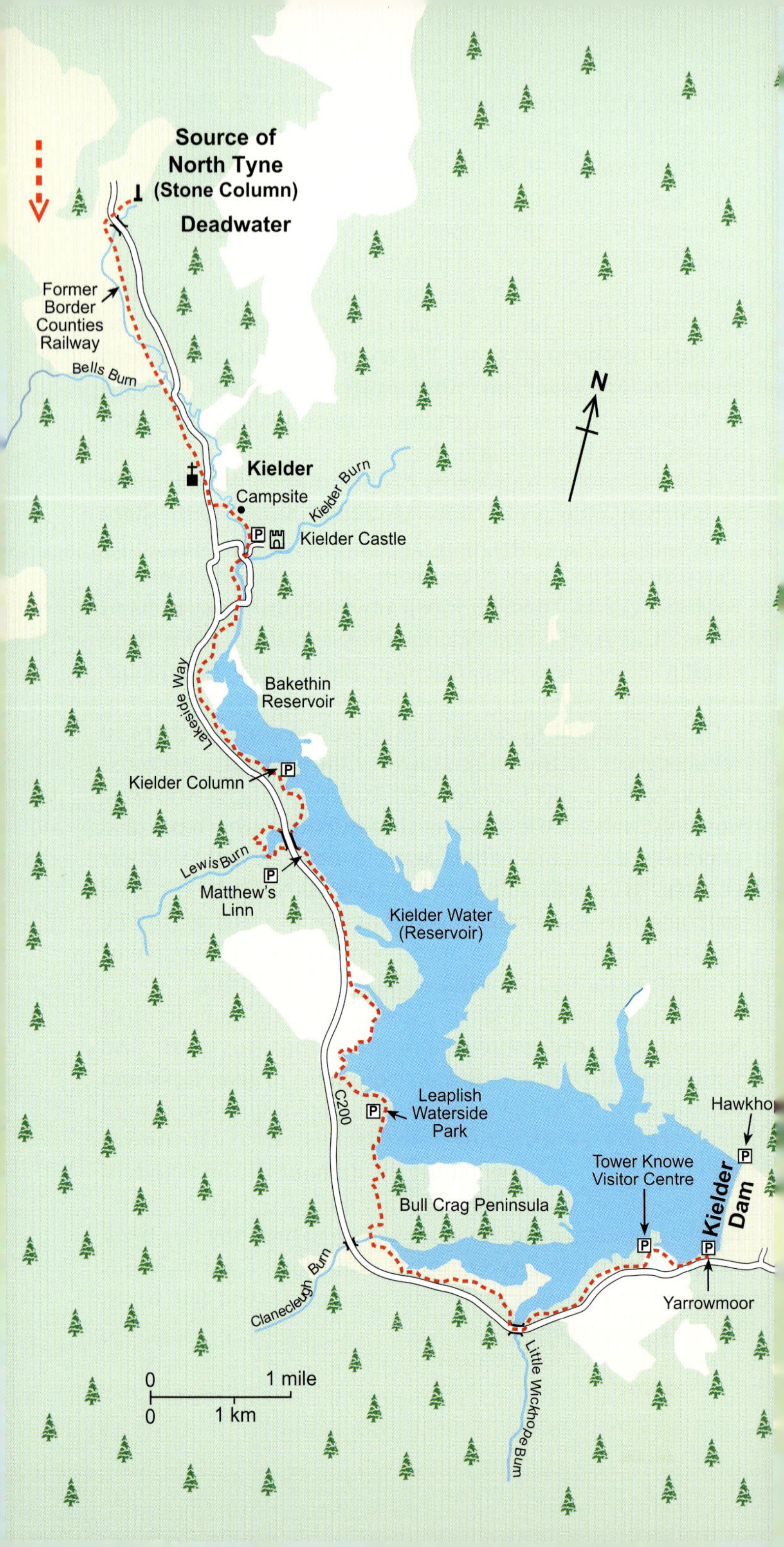

Source of
North Tyne
(Stone Column)
Deadwater
Former
Border
Counties
Railway
Bells Burn
Kielder
Campsite
Kielder Burn
Kielder Castle
N
Bakethin
Reservoir
Lakeside Way
Kielder Column
Lewis Burn
Matthew's
Linn
Kielder Water
(Reservoir)
Leaplish
Waterside
Park
C200
Bull Crag Peninsula
Tower Knowe
Visitor Centre
Kielder
Dam
Hawkho
Yarrowmoor
Clanecleugh Burn
Little Wickhope Burn
0
1 mile
0
1 km

STAGE 1
Source of the North Tyne to the Kielder Dam

15½ miles (25 km)

The trail begins at **Deadwater** where a massive stone sculpture, indicating the source of the North Tyne, stands on the hillside very close to the border between England and Scotland. There is some debate as to the precise location of the source of the North Tyne, however, local farmer Jimmy Hall states that the nearby spring is the only one that never runs dry. It is hard to believe that the tiny trickle of water that emerges will mature into a fast flowing river. The route soon joins the dismantled line of a former railway as you walk on the level, never very far from the infant river, through open country in this sparsely-populated part of England's most northerly county. After 3½ miles you reach Kielder Village and its Kielder Castle Visitor Centre. From here your journey takes you 12 miles along the south shore of Kielder Water.

This is the longest stage of the trail and you need to bear in mind that it is the only one that doesn't end in a town or village. Nevertheless, there are car parks and two visitor centres on route which could facilitate dividing it into shorter sections. You also need to be aware that mobile

Entry/exit points	**Roadside on C200 (GR604974) at the England-Scotland Border some 250yds beyond Deadwater Farm; Kielder 3½ miles (5.6km); Matthew's Linn 7¾ miles (12.5km); Leaplish 10 miles (16km); Tower Knowe 14¾ miles (23.7km); Kielder Dam (Yarrowmoor car park) 15½ miles (25km)**
Map	**OS Outdoor Leisure 42 Kielder Water and Forest**
Refreshments	**The Anglers Arms pub and Kielder Castle Visitor Centre at Kielder Village; visitor centres at Leaplish and Tower Knowe**

Deadwater

Deadwater is a small settlement of neighbouring farms and cottages. It has been suggested that this was the site of a deserted medieval village but no evidence has come to light to verify this. Deadwater Farm lies at the foot of the 1900 ft (579m) Deadwater Fell which sits astride the English-Scottish border. The fell's summit has a military radar installation which is a prominent landmark for miles around and you may well become aware of fighter planes close overhead!

Walking and mountain bike trails from Kielder provide challenges to those aiming to get to the top to enjoy its magnificent views. Here, they can appreciate David Adjaye's artwork *Specere* (2009) which doubles as a shelter.

phone reception is, at best, intermittent. Another thing, don't be fooled into expecting that the waterside path will be flat - on the contrary, be prepared for lots of ups and downs, some of which are fairly steep. Compensation comes in the form of some great views before you arrive at the Kielder Dam. Finally, when Brian Burnie undertook the pilot walk along the Tyne, he was fascinated by the number of crossings along its entire length. With this in mind, reference has been made to the number in each stage of the trail. Although you will not encounter all of them, on this stage of the trail there are twelve crossings (road, pedestrian and railway).

The walk

At the roadside gate you will obtain your first sight and sound of the infant river as it reaches the culvert that takes it under the road. To start the trail, you need to climb the short way up to the stone sculpture by Gilbert Ward (2013) which marks the source of the North Tyne. By permission of Jimmy and Fiona Hall, the only access to the sculpture is

Source of North Tyne
(Photograph: Graeme Peacock)

via the designated path across their land and dogs must be kept under control and gates closed.

(If for any reason the paths on either side of the road should be closed, walk back along the road, go down the track opposite Deadwater Farm and then turn left onto the former railway line-see below).

Follow the path to the obelisk which was lowered by Chinook helicopter in October 2013. If you walk a few paces to the right and look down (but don't descend) the bankside, close to the stone post, you should just be able to see the tiny spring that will grow into a mighty river. As you retrace your steps down the path if you look over to the left you may notice some wooden planks which provide access for the farmer – the first river crossing!

Once through the gate, you will notice how a culvert takes the growing stream beneath the road (the second crossing!). Cross the road with care as it is much used by timber haulage vehicles. Go through the gate and carry on (again by permission of Jimmy and Fiona Hall under the same conditions as above). Go through a further gate and cross a narrow strip of land,

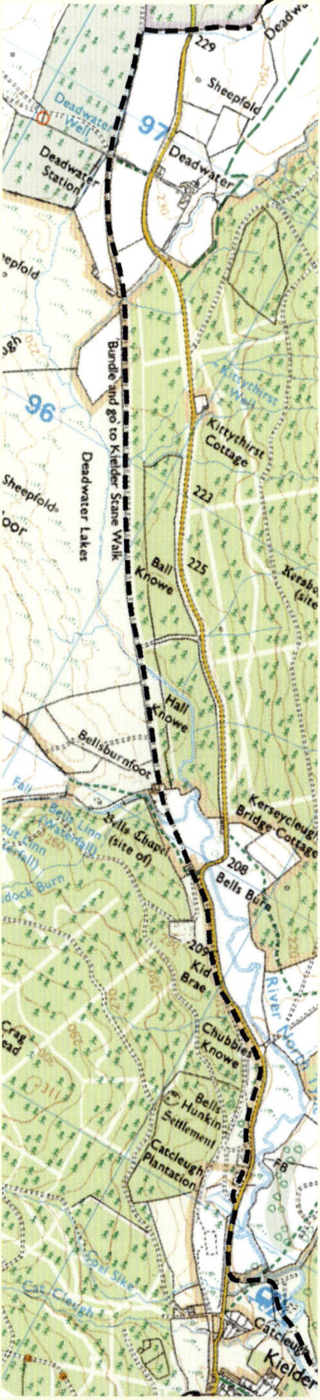

Border Counties Railway

This 42-mile single track line was completed in 1862. It ran from near Hexham in Northumberland to Riccarton Junction in the Scottish Border county of Roxburghshire. It finally closed in 1958. One important aspect was the links with other parts of the rapidly developing rail network: at Hexham with the Newcastle to Carlisle Railway; at Riccarton Junction with the Border Union Railway, with connections to Hawick and Edinburgh; at Reedsmouth Station with the Wansbeck Railway to Morpeth. In addition, at Plashetts there was a link with the Plashetts Colliery Waggonway.

The coming of the railway must have been a real boon to the folk of the North Tyne valley, with provision of passenger and goods services and opportunities for easier contact with the outside world. With 15 stations between Hexham and the Scottish border, the line was readily accessible for most people. It must have taken someone with clout to persuade the company to build a station at sparsely-populated Deadwater!

courtesy of Andrew Douglas, to reach the former Border Counties Railway. Turn left to begin to follow the Foresty Commission's 'Borderline - Kielder Village - Shared Trail' (again dogs must be controlled and gates closed).

Back to England

Although the first waymark post says, "Welcome to England", it would seem, technically at least, that you may be in Scotland until you reach the next gateway! When you reach a gateway, you will see, on your left, the slowly growing rivulet joined by a drainage channel. You are now crossing (!) the nascent North Tyne as it bears off to weave its way through the reeds. Continue ahead and pass the former Deadwater Station, now a private residence. At a gate you

First road bridge (*Photograph: Richard Page*)

cross the Deadwater Burn, which will add considerably to the gradually developing North Tyne. After a further ¾ mile just after a track comes in from the left, you cross a bridge where you can admire the North Tyne now as a definite stream. However, it quickly disappears from view only leaving you to speculate on its progress. You go through a gate and pass Bellsburn Foot Cottage. A short way further on, a bridge crosses the Bells Burn itself as it zig-zags to add to the river. As you proceed ahead, the North Tyne comes clearly into sight as it passes under a fine road bridge.

OS © Crown Copyright 2015 FL-GV100032058

Continue ahead on the track parallel to the road and at a junction of paths, bear left along the broad path to meet the road. On the left is the former Presbyterian chapel of 1874, now the URC Church in association with the Methodist Church. Turn right and walk up the road with care for a short way before turning left to follow the sign to Kielder Camp Site. You cross another bridge over the growing North Tyne and pass the reception office where there is a 'Welcome to Kielder Forest' map. As you carry on, you get close to the tree-lined river before passing The Anglers Arms pub and arriving at a junction. To continue the walk you will be turning right.

Nevertheless, you may wish to turn left and make your way uphill a short way to the visitor centre at **Kielder** (Kielder Castle), where there is a café and an exhibition room. During the appropriate season, a television in the café shows live pictures of nesting ospreys.

The way to follow

Kielder Castle (*Photograph: Graeme Peacock*)

Kielder

Kielder Castle was built in 1775 as a shooting lodge for the 1st Duke of Northumberland. It was reported that the Duke described the local men as savages! Apart from ongoing farming, nothing much disturbed this lonely place until the construction of the Kielder Viaduct in 1862. The 4th Duke insisted that the viaduct was topped with battlements to match his nearby castle. The first trees of what was to become Kielder Forest were planted in the late 1920s. By the 1950s, the growth in afforestation necessitated the building, by the Forestry Commission, of Kielder Village to provide accommodation for forestry workers. With a coverage of 250 square miles, the forest is the largest man-made woodland in Europe. A major project, the construction of Kielder Dam, was completed in 1981 and it took two years for the water to fill the valley behind the dam to become Kielder Water. This is the UK's largest man-made reservoir by capacity (200 billion litres).

Both the forest and the reservoir have experienced changes to their original objectives: the creation of a strategic reserve of growing timber and as a supplier of water to the North East respectively. They have also become integral parts of Kielder Water and Forest Park which promotes tourism as a vital element of the local economy. The Kielder fish hatchery has made a significant contribution in establishing the Tyne as the premier salmon fishing river in England and Wales.

To continue from the junction after the Anglers Arms, turn right, walk across the bridge over the North Tyne and proceed to the main road. Turn left and then right to pick up the Lakeside Way path. However, first of all you may wish to walk a few yards ahead to the bridge where on the left you can see the confluence of the North Tyne and the Kielder Burn.

The riverside path leads to a road with Butteryhaugh Bridge to your left. Cross straight over the road in the direction 'Kielder Viaduct'. After a short distance, turn right at the fingerpost 'LSW South Shore: Kielder Viaduct'.

The path takes you between two large boulders and then climbs steadily to the top of the rise. At the junction of paths continue straight ahead. (The path to the left leads to the splendid **Kielder Viaduct** which is worth visiting if time allows.)

The path curves to the left and joins a surfaced track. Continue down the track a short way and then turn right at a further sign for Lakeside Way South Shore. When you reach a fork, bear right at the boulder and continue on the surfaced track. Keep on the forest path and eventually Kielder Water comes into view.

You will now have walked about 4½ miles from the source of the North Tyne. The river has been subsumed within the vast body of water that you will follow for the next 11 miles until the river is reconstituted as water is released from the

Kielder Water Forest *(Photograph: Graeme Peacock)*

dam. As you proceed, the outline of Bakethin Weir may just become visible ahead in the form of concrete structures jutting out from each side of the shore. This weir has made

Kielder Viaduct

This magnificent structure, which carried the Border Counties Railway over the North Tyne, was completed in 1862. Its battlemented top and mock arrow slits were incorporated to comply with the Duke of Northumberland's request for it to complement nearby Kielder Castle. Because it crossed the river at an angle it was erected as a skew-arch; a plaque credits the Newcastle geometrician, Peter Nicholson, with setting out the principles for this method of construction.

Following the closure of the railway in 1958, the viaduct fell into disuse and was later owned by the Forestry Commission which decided to demolish it. Fortunately, it was saved by the Northumberland and Newcastle Society, which acquired it for a nominal sum and later arranged for waterproofing of the deck and concrete casings for the bases. In 2004 the Society and the Kielder Community Trust commissioned the production of eight iron panels which are set between parapets. A short stroll across this scheduled ancient monument enables you enjoy the panels as well as the splendid views of man-made Kielder Water.

OS © Crown Copyright 2015 FL-GV100032058

the water level in this area of Kielder like a natural lake and so it attracts a great variety of wildlife.

Frequent Lakeside Way South Shore signs will clearly mark your route from here onwards. As you continue, your ultimate destination, the Kielder Dam, will be indicated, as will be intermediate points such as Leaplish and Tower Knowe. However, don't be alarmed if the dam appears to be such a long way as you will be taking an alternative route to avoid Bull Crag, which will save you some 3 miles after Leaplish!

You meet a metalled road at a small car park area where you turn left and then right (unless you wish to see the *Kielder Column*). Now continue ahead and follow the track as it bears left just before the art work *Mirage* (an ideal spot to rest and admire the view!).

OS © Crown Copyright 2015 FL-GV100032058

You pass under the C200 road bridge as the path begins a ¾ mile loop around a long inlet from the Lewis Burn. You can rest and admire the view at Pattterson's Pause. You cross a neatly curved bridge before you eventually return to the lakeside.

You arrive at a car park at Matthew's Linn with the Calvert Trust activity centre and toilets on your left. After a further ½ mile, you bear right onto a surface track and then turn left onto a shared road which passes the access to Hawkhirst Scout Activity Centre, opened in 1982 when the valley was flooded. The track takes you through a gate after which you turn right and cross the Hawkhirst Burn. The trail then winds its way to Leaplish through the car park area with the amenities of the visitor centre on your left, which you may want to explore.

However, to continue, proceed a short way on the road past the visitor centre then turn left onto the Lakeside Way. Follow the tree-lined path back towards the lakeside and at a junction of paths don't take the squirrel hide route, unless you're particularly keen on squirrels, instead turn right. The path descends to the lakeside and you pass the Kielder Water Ski Club on your left.

Steady climb

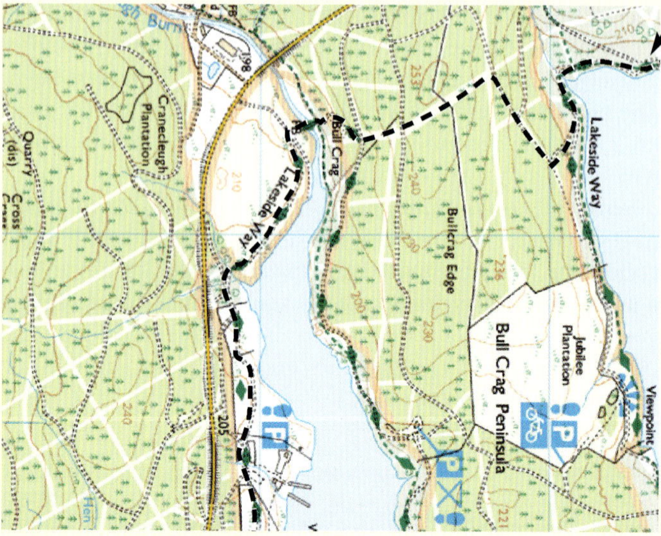

Continue ahead until you arrive at a welcome sign indicating that you turn right onto the alternative route (thus avoiding the additional 3 miles around Bull Crag) to Tower Knowe. The path climbs to Freya's Cabin where you can enjoy both the story and the view across to Robin's cabin. Continue climbing for several hundred yards before dropping down to a junction. Turn right, walk about 100yds and then turn left. Follow the track between the trees until a sign directs you to the right. The path zig-zags down before crossing the Clanecleugh Burn and then climbs equally steeply. You will soon have good views across the bay towards the Bull Crag Peninsula and you

OS © Crown Copyright 2015 FL-GV100032058

can appreciate what you have avoided!

Ignore any paths or roads off as the Lakeside Way path leads you on towards the dam. The trail skirts the woods with their fine array of towering trees and you cross an access road that leads to the Kielder Yacht Club. You go over a further tributary (Little Whickhope Burn) before you climb past an access road at the entrance to the Outdoor Education Centre. You begin to wonder if you will ever reach your destination but suddenly you find the visitor centre at Tower Knowe on your left, your last opportunity for an ice cream or a cup of tea! The path continues ahead between the trees and soon you'll be pleased to know that the end is literally in sight as you walk the remaining ¾ mile or so to the Yarrowmoor car park, the Kielder Dam and the end of this stage of the Daft as a Brush Cancer Patient Care Walk.

End of Stage 1

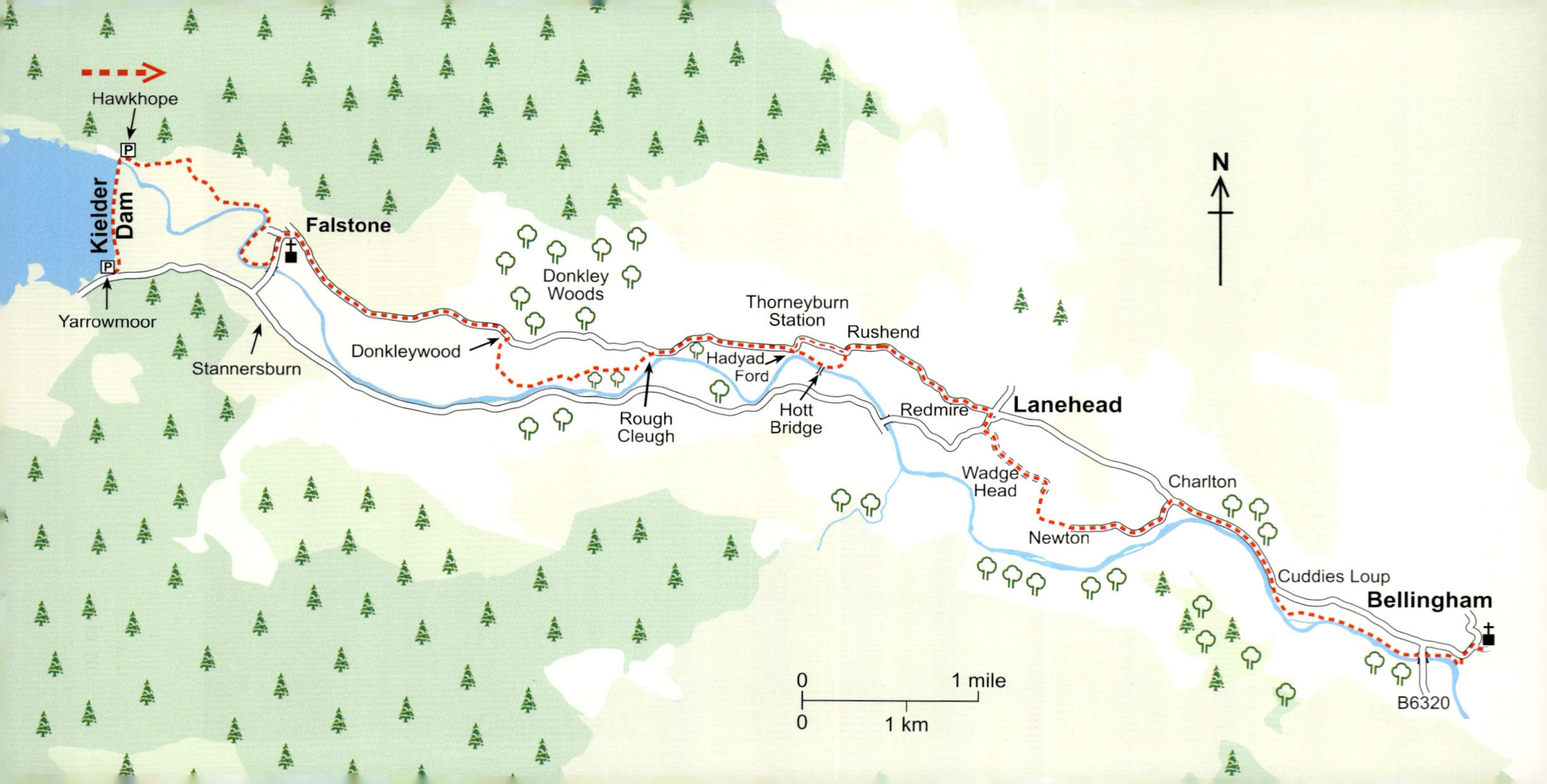
Hawkhope
Kielder Dam
Yarrowmoor
Falstone
Stannersburn
Donkleywood
Donkley Woods
Thorneyburn Station
Rushend
Hadyad Ford
Hott Bridge
Rough Cleugh
Redmire
Lanehead
Wadge Head
Newton
Charlton
Cuddies Loup
Bellingham
B6320
N
0
1 mile
0
1 km

STAGE 2

Kielder Dam to Bellingham

12¼ miles (19.7 km)

You begin this stage by walking across the top of the dam from where you can appreciate the emergence of the North Tyne as it recommences its journey towards its meeting with the South Tyne. The route takes you across a mixture of rugged moorland, meadow lands and tree-lined riverside paths. This stage contains an amount of road walking along quiet minor roads and farm tracks and with about a mile on a more major road. However, the North Tyne is never far away and there are significant stretches to enjoy close to the river. You can expect to climb quite steeply at times before benefitting from the equally lengthy descents. You are accompanied on a large part of your journey by the vestiges of the former Border Counties Railway line. There are five river crossings on this stage of the trail. After crossing the North Tyne via the dam, you remain on the north side of the river where you pass close to three crossings and go beneath a road bridge.

Entry/exit points	**Yarrowmoor car park (GR707871); Falstone 2 miles (3.2km); Lanehead 8 miles (12.9km); Bellingham 12¼ miles (19.7km)**
Map	**OS Explorer OL42 Kielder Water & Forest**
Refreshments	**Tearoom and hotel in Falstone; range of hotels, pubs and cafés in Bellingham**

The walk

The walk starts close to the Kielder Dam at the Yarrowmoor car park where a fingerpost indicates 'Falstone Village 1¾'. At the nearby Fishing Lodge a further sign suggests, perhaps more accurately, that the distance is 2 miles! Proceed across the Kielder Dam taking advantage of the fine views on either side. The valve tower on the left controls

The river is re-born

the flow of water from the dam, while on your right as you progress, you will catch your first glimpse of the born-again River North Tyne.

Turn right to pass the plaque and the stone monument commemorating the official opening of the dam by HM The Queen in 1982. You join a track which you follow downhill until you reach a sign that directs you to turn right for Falstone. Head towards the farm buildings where you bear left to go through a gate. Continue ahead and cross the

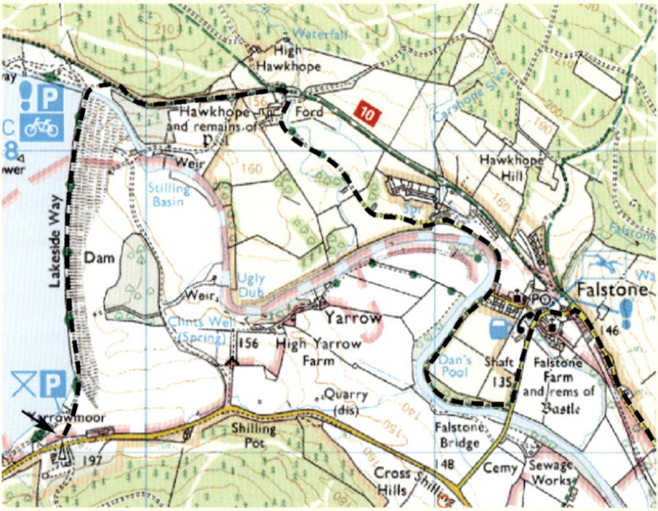

Hawkhope Burn as it makes its circuitous way to join the North Tyne. Proceed along the surfaced road ignoring roads off as the dwellings of Falstone come into view. You are greeted by splendid views of the North Tyne.

The road leads past an attractive children's play area. At the end of the tennis courts, leave the road as it swings left and instead turn right to follow the sign 'Riverside Walk and The Stell'. With the river close by, follow the path to arrive at what looks like a sheepfold but is in fact a sculpture (Colin Wilbourn, 2006). You can relax on the life-like stone cushions and study depictions of local industrial history and lost place names.

To continue, walk ahead. On the left you should soon be able to see parts of Falstone with its tall URC Church. The path makes its way to the road bridge where you bear left. It then runs parallel to the road, goes through a gate and winds through some trees until you exit onto the road and turn left. You pass an information board about the Tynedale

Falstone

This is a very small settlement nestling in the North Tyne Valley amid scattered farmsteads and coniferous forest plantations. Being just a short distance from the major tourist attraction of Kielder Water has led to an increase in passing tourists and walkers. Falstone itself contains a mixture of dwellings including some 1920s Forestry Commission housing. It offers a tearoom with craft gallery, community shop and a visitor information point in the former village school. The Jubilee Drinking Fountain, like the school building, dates from Victorian times and stands a few yards before the tearoom. Architectural design awards were deservingly granted in 2004 when the building was refurbished and adapted for renewable energy usage. Older rugby enthusiasts will be interested to see from a plaque that the tearoom was officially opened by Roger Utley. Across the road is another award winner, the Blackcock Inn and Restaurant. Falstone's two other significant buildings are: the URC Church (originally Presbyterian, dating from 1709 and modified in 1807 and 1876) and now serving in association with the Methodists; and St Peter's Church which is believed to be near the site of a medieval chapel. However, the current church of 1882 is largely the replacement of that of 1824 which was badly damaged by fire.

Approaching Falstone

Renewable Energy Trail. Follow the road as it goes between the Tearoom and the Blackcock Inn. It then passes St Peter's Church before going under a former railway bridge and reaching a junction.

To continue on the trail, bear right at the junction and keep straight ahead on the road for the next 1¾ miles. It is more like a narrow lane and hopefully you are unlikely to be disturbed by any more than the odd farm vehicle while the grass verge gives you adequate sanctuary. You pass reminders of the old railway in the form of Station House, Station Cottage, and the Waiting Room. The road climbs gradually and you reach open countryside. It is worth stopping from time to time to get your breath and to look behind where the dam and the valve tower remain in sight for some time. Across the valley you can see isolated farmsteads and forested plantations, however, the tree-lined valley below is practically the only indication of the river along this section. You should also be able to pick out the line of the old railway.

After about a mile, as the road descends you should see the site of the old station and the bridge over which you will cross. Eventually you reach the small hamlet of Donkleywood with some farm buildings on your left and a public footpath sign (and a Railway Cottage sign) just before Donkleywood House. Turn right and walk across the grass to go over a ladder stile. Walk between the cottages and proceed through

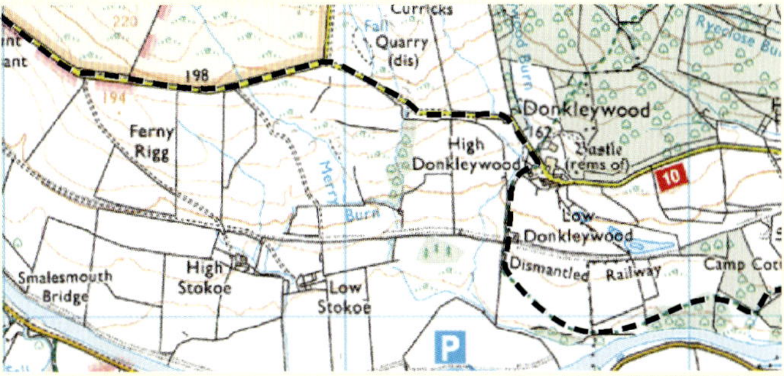

the waymarked gate. Follow the farm track and go over the stone bridge with Railway Cottage (1860) on the left. The track deteriorates somewhat and can be muddy and slippery.

Just before a stone gateway, a waymark directs you to the left. You need to follow the same line diagonally left, heading in the first instance towards a prominent tree that stands some distance, alone, in front of the woods. The ground may be boggy and the path indistinct, but make your way to pass the oak tree on your right. Continue in the same direction, towards the edge of the wood, to the wall at the corner of the field where there is a waymarked stile next to a metal gate.

Cross the stile and turn left. You will be rewarded with your first good views of what is now a wider River North Tyne. Follow the path, which may be overgrown in parts, between the trees. The occasional sound of an engine indicates that there is a road on the other side of the river. As you climb away from the river, the path follows the line of a wire fence on your left. You cross a stile which is waymarked (as is practically the whole of this stage of the trail).

Climbing away from the river

The path keeps roughly about 15yds from the now heightened fence and eventually leads through a wooden gate. After going over another stile, make for a waymarked post at the right-hand end of the stone wall. Continue ahead as indicated and at the end of the property (Camp Cottage) bear right to make for a stile a few paces to the left of a wide gate. After crossing the stile, bear right in the direction of the waymark and walk across the field. There is no clear path so look out for a stile on the right, a short distance before the field corner, next to a metal gate. You'll be pleased to know there's a waymark here, although it does happen to be on the step!

Go over the stile and keep near the fence on your left as the path descends. You may have to negotiate a small burn before following the fence as it turns left. Climb steeply alongside the fence then walk a few steps ahead to meet a fenced area through which a gate on the left-hand side provides access. Pass through another gate. Now continue with a fence on your right as the river reappears. Go over the stile in the left-hand corner (again the waymark is on the step).

Below is a stream, the Rough Cleugh, over which there is a small footbridge. 'Rough' seems a very appropriate word as both banksides can be slippery and considerable care needs to be taken. You need to clamber down to reach the footbridge. Once over the bridge, bear left and then climb to the right to cross a stile in the fence above. Turn right on the narrow road on which you started this stage of your journey.

Follow the road for just over ¾ mile with traces of the old railway on your left. You pass farm buildings and some fine properties. Eventually the road climbs, the river re-emerges and you reach a corner (Hadyad Ford) where the road bears left. On the right a finger-post indicates, 'The Hott ½'. Here you have a choice of routes for the next ½ mile: either, **(A)** continue along the road, or **(B)** leave the road to walk along the riverside past the Hott Bridge.

(A): This route continues on the narrow quiet road with two gates to open and close.

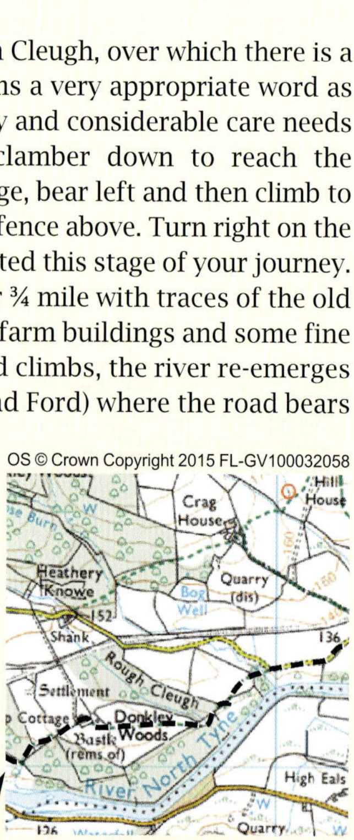

Hott Bridge

Proceed along the road past the former Thorneyburn Station (1861-1956) gatekeeper's cottage and crossing gates. After just under ½ mile, at a sharp left-hand bend, on your right, you will see a fingerpost, 'The Hott ½', next to a ladder stile in a wall. At this point you have arrived at the point at which route (B) re-joins the road.

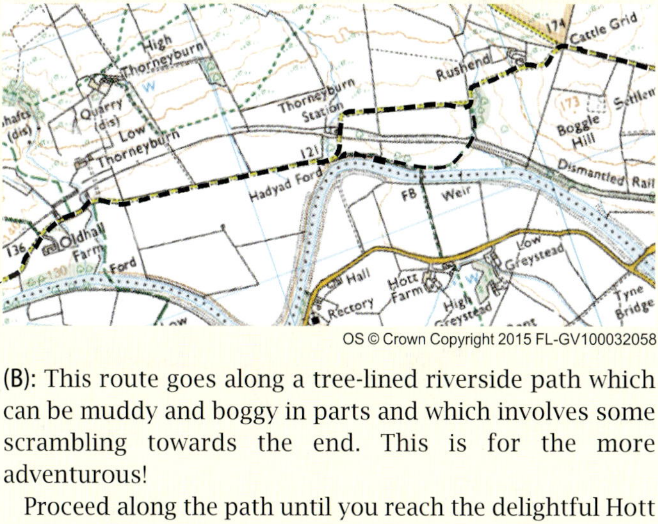

(B): This route goes along a tree-lined riverside path which can be muddy and boggy in parts and which involves some scrambling towards the end. This is for the more adventurous!

Proceed along the path until you reach the delightful Hott Bridge, built in 1862 to provide access to Thorneyburn Station from Hott Farm, High and Low Greystead. It is worth climbing the stone steps to the suspension bridge in order to view the river. Walk past the bridge for about 100yds. Then bear left to follow a faint track up the rise where you will see the old railway embankment ahead. Bear right to make for a tunnel under the old line. Pass through the short low underpass and exit by a gate. The ground ahead is usually marshy and rutted due to the cattle that sometimes gather here. You need to bear left and climb to a small waymarked post. Now continue ahead, bearing right in the direction of the waymark, to reach a ladder stile, next to a fingerpost, in the right-hand corner of the field. Cross the stile and enjoy the relief of getting back onto the road where you might even meet some friends who preferred the easier (but more boring) Route **(A)** past Thorneyburn Station.

Now continue along the quiet road which soon crosses the stone bridge over the Lairney Burn. The road then climbs steeply past Rushend. At its highest point, the road arrives at a cattle grid and a junction. Here you can get your breath back and look back to admire the fine view. Having gained height you now descend for about ½ mile and cross the Tarset Burn.

(The Tarset Burn is an attractive waterway flowing south to join the North Tyne. A short distance to the west of the confluence of the two rivers stands another 'Tyne Bridge' sometimes referred to as the Tarset Tyne Bridge.)

Continue climbing to pass Redmire as you make your way to the junction at Lanehead. Just before the junction you pass the eco-friendly Tarset Tor Backpackers which opened in 2013. At the junction turn right and walk down the side of the road for about 150yds. This is a busier road and you may need to use the grass verge from time to time. On your

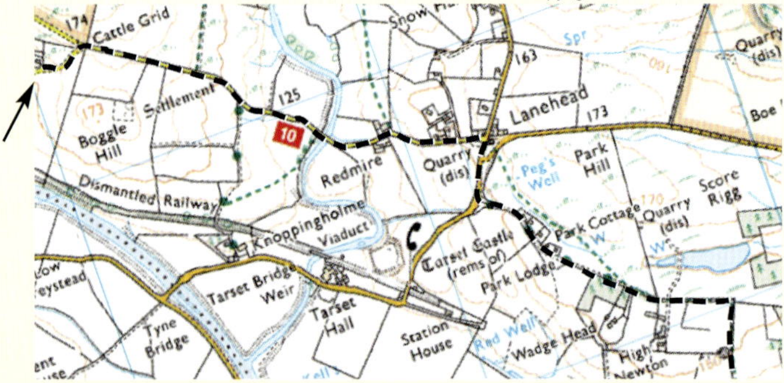

Near Lanehead

left, you first pass a road to Newcastle, Hexham and Bellingham before crossing over with care near a corner to go along a minor road.

Proceed along this very quiet road passing a few dwellings including Tyne View from where you might just about catch a glimpse of the North Tyne. The road leads past a wood and the entrance to a property (Wadge Head), while ahead to the left you can see a pond. You pass a cattle grid and the road surface deteriorates somewhat. Keep straight ahead. The road reaches a corner where it turns sharply right before coming to an end at the entrance to a dwelling on the right.

Carry on through the waymarked gateway and walk straight down the field. Turn left at the corner of the field

to arrive at a bridge that once carried the railway. Turn right under the bridge where the path may be muddy. Turn immediately left to pass a cluster of farm building and fine properties at Newton. Once beyond the buildings you continue along a relatively-recently tree-lined driveway. The road stretches through pleasant meadow land, bearing right at Charltongate before arriving at a T-junction at Charlton.

Turn right to proceed along this much busier road for about a mile. Take great care along here. You may need to take refuge on what is at first a narrow verge but which happily widens out about half-way along. As the road bends sharply to the left, you will be relieved to leave it and cross a waymarked stile on the right to pick up the public footpath 'Bellingham 1 mile'.

Follow the path, known as Cuddies Loup (Cuddy being a nickname for (St) Cuthbert whose ancient well you will pass). Keep close to the bankside and along the field edge. Resist any temptation to enter the woods and instead follow the embankment with a wire fence and woods on your right. At the end of the woods, at a sign 'Danger Cast with Care', bear right to return to the bankside and enjoy the river views. The path becomes delightfully tree-lined. It crosses a small burn. You go through a kissing gate. After the second gate, you will see a cricket field, behind which is the Riverdale Hall Hotel, as the buildings of **Bellingham** come into view. You go through a third gate and then you

Approaching Bellingham on Cuddies Loup

OS © Crown Copyright 2015 FL-GV100032058

walk under a river crossing in the form of the Bellingham Road Bridge. You pass a broad green area with picnic tables as you continue ahead on the hard surface path that leads into Bellingham. Conveniently placed benches provide an opportunity to enjoy views of the majestic sweep of the river.

You arrive at a garage (Riverside Garage). Immediately opposite, on the left, a path leads to St Cuthbert's Well, beyond which are steps that lead to the church named after the saint. However, to continue, you need to walk a few paces past the garage, where a fingerpost indicates that you have reached the junction of the north and south riverside walks. You will head south from here on the next stage of the walk to Barrasford. Meanwhile, turn left and walk up to

Cuddy's Well

the fine Boer War Memorial close to the Rose & Crown pub and the walker-friendly Rocky Road café. You have now come to the end of this stage of the Daft as Brush Cancer Patient Care Walk.

Arriving in Bellingham

Bellingham

The former market town of Bellingham and 'Capital of the North Tyne', is an important centre for smaller local communities. A little less so, perhaps, since the closure of Bellingham Auction Mart in 2009. Happily, the end of August annual agricultural show, now designated 'Bellingham Show and Country Festival' continues. Bellingham is a popular centre for cyclists and walkers; the Pennine Way passes through the town. A pleasant 3 mile walk is to the 30ft (9m) waterfall, Hareshaw Linn. In the 19th century, Hareshaw Dene, the valley leading to the fall, was the centre of iron working, but is now a peaceful spot and a Site of Special Scientific Interest.

St Cuthbert's Church dates back to at least the 12th century and is noted for its unique vaulted stone roof – possibly a wise fire precaution in the days of marauding Scots! The dedication to the Northumbrian St Cuthbert (AD 634-687) fits in with the claim that this was one of the many places where the saint's body rested on its journey to its final resting place in what is now Durham Cathedral. Below the church, St

Cuthbert's Well (Cuddy's Well) is said to have had miraculous powers. Some traditions suggest that Cuthbert, having discovered the well, used its waters to baptise his early converts. The water has certainly been used in more recent times for baptisms in the church. The 'Long Pack' tombstone in the graveyard is a reminder of a legend of an attempted felony with a tragic ending. Further tourist information and cultural insights can be found at the Tourist Information Centre located at The Heritage Centre at Station House, Station Yard where there is a fascinating museum as well as a tearoom.

Bellingham *(Photograph: Graeme Peacock)*

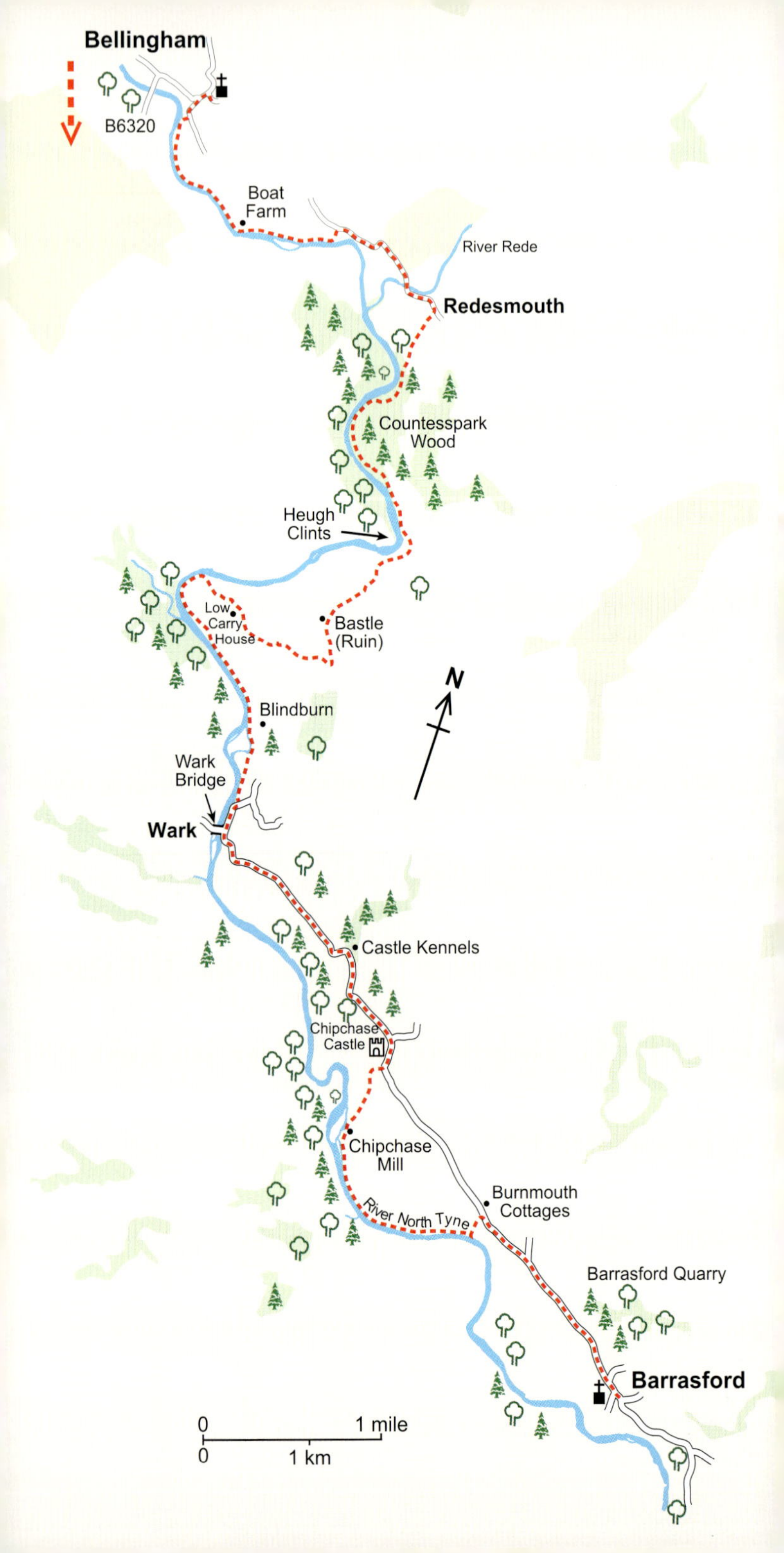

Bellingham
B6320
Boat
Farm
River Rede
Redesmouth
Countesspark
Wood
Heugh
Clints
Low
Carry
House
Bastle
(Ruin)
N
Blindburn
Wark
Bridge
Wark
Castle Kennels
Chipchase
Castle
Chipchase
Mill
River North Tyne
Burnmouth
Cottages
Barrasford Quarry
Barrasford
0
1 mile
0
1 km

STAGE 3
Bellingham to Barrasford
13¼ miles (21.3 km)

This walk covers a wide variety of terrains. You walk along delightful riverside and woodland paths and you use two short sections of the old Border Counties Railway. The trail crosses some rough moorland before following a farm track that leads back to the riverside where you walk along the riverbank opposite the village of Wark. This is followed by about 1½ miles on a quiet minor road leading past Chipchase Castle. A track goes alongside the river through an important fishing area before returning to the road for a further mile into Barrasford. There are several climbs and following heavy rain some areas can be quite muddy. There is only one river crossing, that at Wark, which you don't go over unless you are seeking refreshments.

Entry/exit points	**Bellingham (GR839834); Wark 8.25 miles (13.3km); Barrasford 13¼ miles (21.3km)**
Maps	**OS Explorers OL42 Kielder Water & Forest; OL43 Hadrian's Wall**
Refreshments	**Cafés and pubs in Bellingham; pubs and hotel in Wark; village shop and hotel in Barrasford**

The Walk
From the Boer War Memorial, close to the Rose & Crown pub and the Rocky Road café, walk downhill to the Riverside Garage. Here the road forks and you bear left in the direction 'Riverside Walk (South)'. Cross the bridge over the Hareshaw Burn and turn immediately right in the direction of the finger post 'Boat 1'. Follow the path to where the burn enters the North Tyne. The path is carefully directed past a large property. The tree-lined path passes through a gate and you continue ahead along the riverbank with pasture land on the left. Go through a kissing gate and walk between the trees. Depending on the season, the path can be

Leaving Bellingham

somewhat overgrown and/or muddy, although some duck-boarding certainly helps.

After just less than a mile, the path leaves the riverside through a kissing gate to join an access road. Turn right and walk between two cottages at Boat. The road leads to The Boat Farm where you pass some holiday cottages and the river comes back into view. Gates take you across two fields close to the river, after which a faded waymark directs you to climb left up a farm track to a gate. Go through the gate onto the road and turn right.

Follow the generally quiet road for about ½ mile. Initially there is no verge so extra care is needed; be particularly

aware of the traffic while walking beneath a railway bridge. There is open moorland on your left and you will find a railway embankment on your right. You cross a bridge over the River Rede, a further important tributary of the North Tyne. The piers of an earlier railway bridge are clearly visible.

Continue alongside the road as it climbs quite steeply, being prepared to use the left hand-side at sharp corners. At the top of the rise, a fingerpost on the left indicates your next destination 'Countess Park Wood ½'. Turn immediately right onto the access road between the dwellings of the hamlet of Redesmouth. You soon reach a public foot-path sign 'Birtley 3' at a

Old and new crossings of the Rede

junction of paths at the corner of a field. The right of way has been officially redirected from this point.

Go through the kissing gate, turn left and proceed ahead close to the fence to reach a waymark post. Now go diagonally right to pick up a faint path towards the far corner of the field. Descend near the corner of a platform of the old Redesmouth Station to a waymark post to meet the dismantled railway line. Here it can be particularly muddy and rutted. Walk between the platforms and past two former station buildings converted into residential properties, the second of which bears the image of a steam train.

Make your way ahead for several hundred yards as best as you can. You may need to follow local custom and practice and use the embankment to pass a section where cattle tend to graze. You come to a ladder stile on the right (you'll know you've gone too far if the way is blocked by a gate!). Cross the stile, go down the steps onto a narrow path and bear left at the fork. The path is steep at first and again, at times, muddy. You are now in Countesspark Wood.

The path leads to a broad vehicular track which makes progress easier and you are rewarded with views of the river. You pass a wooden cabin. Eventually, as the vehicular track appears to end, continue straight ahead on the narrow path which then bears away from the riverside. You cross a short section of duck-boarding and you climb further from

Countesspark Wood

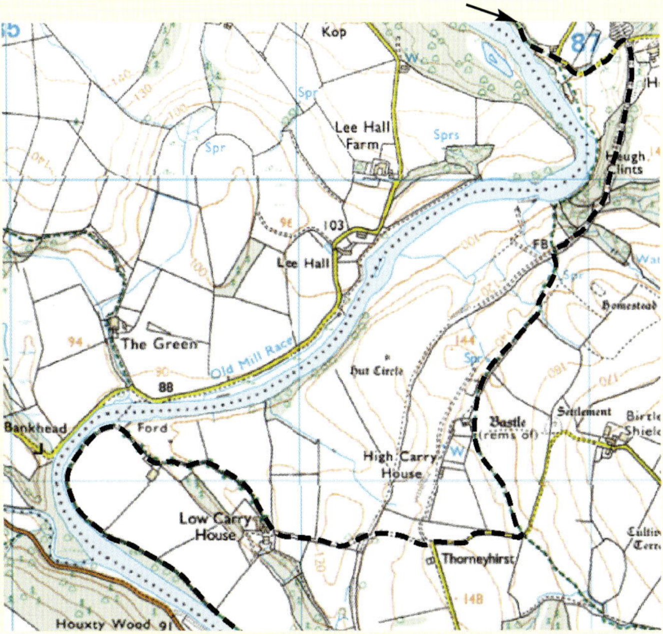

the riverbank. The high path undulates but you remain aware of both the sound and sight of the river below.

You reach a gate. (At the time of writing, a notice advises that, as a result of unstable conditions on the bankside ahead, at Heugh Clints, the path has been redirected along the old railway line.) You climb gently ahead past a pleasant property to an access road. Turn right and follow the road as it descends to a now-culverted ford.

(In the unlikely event of the ford being impassable, turn left instead of right at the access road. Climb up the road, go under the railway bridge and turn sharply to the right to reach the old railway line where you turn left and proceed as above along the tree-lined track.)

Cross the ford and continue on the road as it climbs steeply to pass under a gated bridge. A waymark indicates that the route is immediately to the right up the bankside to a gateway. (If the bankside is wet and slippery, you can walk up the track and then turn sharp right to reach the gateway.) Walk through the gateway to join the old railway track and turn left on the permissive path. Proceed along the tree-lined track until your path is blocked by a metal gate. What a pity that more use can't be made of the former railway!

Turn left as indicated by the waymark and climb the steps to go through a double wooden gate. Note the direction of the waymark as the next ¾ mile is across rough moorland with no clear path and you need to navigate your way carefully with the aid of limited landmarks. Straight ahead is a clump of trees. Climb diagonally right (direction 2 o'clock) keeping equidistant between the clump of trees and the fence down to your right. At the top of the climb, descend to a solitary tree, beyond which is a metal gate in the wire fence.

Former bastle
(*Photograph: Richard Page*)

Go through the gate and climb up the steep bankside to a waymarked post at the corner of a wire fence. Now walk along the wide expanse of uneven grassland with the wire fence on your left. The fence is replaced by a stone wall and you arrive at a ladder stile just before some farm buildings and the remains of a bastle (fortified farmhouse).

Cross the stile and walk a few paces ahead to the corner of the wall near a wooden gate. Bear slightly left towards a distant telegraph pole to the left of a small rocky outcrop. From the pole (which has a small waymark) proceed ahead

in the same direction to find a fingerpost and a gate a short way to the right of a solitary tree. Go through the gate, bear right to cross a ladder stile and join an access road. You can relax now that you have completed the difficult part!

Walk a couple of hundred yards along the access road to a fingerpost at a junction near a large tree. Carry straight ahead on the byway towards Low Carry House. The road makes its way to the entrance to the farm where you turn right as indicated by the waymark. Walk a few paces, go through the waymarked gate and proceed ahead along the track. At the entrance to some barns, turn right to continue on the track, with a hedge on your left, for about 100yds. Bear right towards a fingerpost next to a gate. Go through the gate and turn left in the direction 'Blindburn 1'. You'll be pleased to see that the river reappears!

You pass through a further gate and the narrow riverside path soon joins a broad vehicular-style track which leads into a field. Walk along the field edge with trees on your right to arrive at a waymarked bridleway gate. Go through the gate to join the broader track which takes you alongside the river. You need to leave the track as it bears left towards a large clearing lying a few yards ahead. Here, you bear right onto a narrow path towards the riverside. Continue along the path for about 150yds taking good care to look out for a waymarked gate on your left.

Go through the gate, turn right and walk ahead close

Across to Wark *(Photograph: Graeme Peacock)*

to the fence on your right. Ignore an old gate on the right. Continue over the fields through the way-marked gates. Eventually you pass some stables on your left. The track soon joins a metalled road and you pass the road entrance to Blindburn. A road comes in from the left and the village of Wark comes into view across the river. Benches on the riverside provide an opportunity for a well-earned rest!

You arrive at Wark Bridge (1878 – substantially renovated 2013-14). You now need to walk along the road for about 2 miles. The road is relatively quiet and there is a reasonable grass verge when required. The road takes you past the sports ground, outlying properties and cultivated fields.

Eventually you reach some wooded areas. You pass the entrance to Castle Kennels and then, on your right, the stone wall of the castle grounds. You come to the entrance to Chipchase Castle Gardens and Nursery and then, as the road bears right, you pass the fine gateway to **Chipchase Castle** itself.

Chipchase Castle

The castle combines a 14th century tower with a 17th century mansion and subsequent adaptations, which, together, present a dignified, pleasing wholeness. As you walk towards Chipchase Mill, you are rewarded with splendid views of this most photogenic building standing on a high point above the river. Sir Peter de Insula was the first recorded owner of the Chipchase estate, which passed to the Heron family on the marriage of Sir Peter's female descendent, Cecily. The estate remained in the ownership of the Herons for 350 years, although by the end of the 18th century, owing to land disposals, it had been reduced in size to the castle and the immediate surrounding area. Subsequently, there were a number of owners until the estate was acquired in 1862 by Mr Hugh Taylor, whose descendants still own and run the estate.

Chipchase Castle has facilities for shooting, fishing, and other events. It is open to the public daily from 1st to 28th June (2.00 pm to 5.00 pm). The grounds and nursery are open from Easter to 31st August. Opening times are shown at the garden entrance.

Chipchase Castle

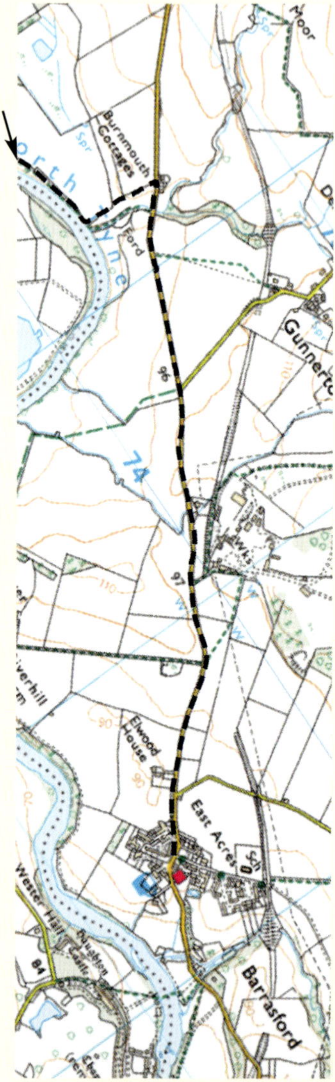

After a further couple of hundred yards from the castle entrance, make sure to turn right and join the signposted access road to Chipchase Mill. There is a post box on the left. In a short distance, to the right, you can enjoy a splendid view of the castle and the adjacent chapel. Continuing ahead downhill you pass the holiday cottage and farm buildings at Chipchase Mill on your left.

After a while you can appreciate the sound and sight of the river. Chipchase is a noted salmon fishing area so don't be surprised to see folk in waders or on their private benches. You pass an access track to Chipchase Strother Cottage. Continue ahead until the broad track ends at a turning area. Carry straight on along the narrow path, which can become very overgrown at times, until the path turns away from the river and reaches some rows of young trees. (Originally the right of way continued ahead to cross a stream at a ford which is now impassable. What follows is currently a permissive path.) Bear left and walk a short distance between the young trees to join a wider track that swings to the right and turns left to climb through a gateway onto a road at Burnmouth Cottages.

Turn right and walk along the road which may be slightly busier but there is a verge on which to seek refuge when required. Barrasford lies about 1½ miles ahead. Ignore signs off. When you reach a nice property on the left with white fencing, you will be pleased to find a path alongside the verge that leads all the way to Barrasford. You pass the entrance to Lafarge Tarmac Barrasford Quarry. At W.G Grieve and Son Garage, cross over to use the pavement on the right-hand side of the road. You reach a road junction. The Methodist Chapel is on the corner and the Village Shop is a few yards further along the side road. Continue a short distance along the main road to the bus shelter on the left, with the Barrasford Arms a little way ahead. You have now completed this stage of the Daft as a Brush Cancer Patient Care Walk.

Barrasford

Barrasford is a small, attractive Northumbrian village. Evidence of its antiquity is found in nearby Iron Age and Romano-British settlements. Between 1860 and 1956 the village had its own railway station on the Border Counties line. Among other things, the railway was extremely useful to Barrasford Quarry, which remains an important part of the local economy. A large sanatorium to treat TB patients, located between Barrasford and the neighbouring village of Gunnerton, was open from 1907 until 1960. Sadly, a fire destroyed the building after the sanatorium closed. However, a recent heritage project includes details of life in the sanatorium. There is not a parish church in the village but Barrasford Methodist Chapel has served the community since 1878. Unusually for Methodist chapels, it has adopted the practice of calling its congregation to services by the ringing of a bell. The Barrrasford Arms is a well-known local hostelry and the Barrasford Village Shop satisfies a range of needs.

Local hostelry

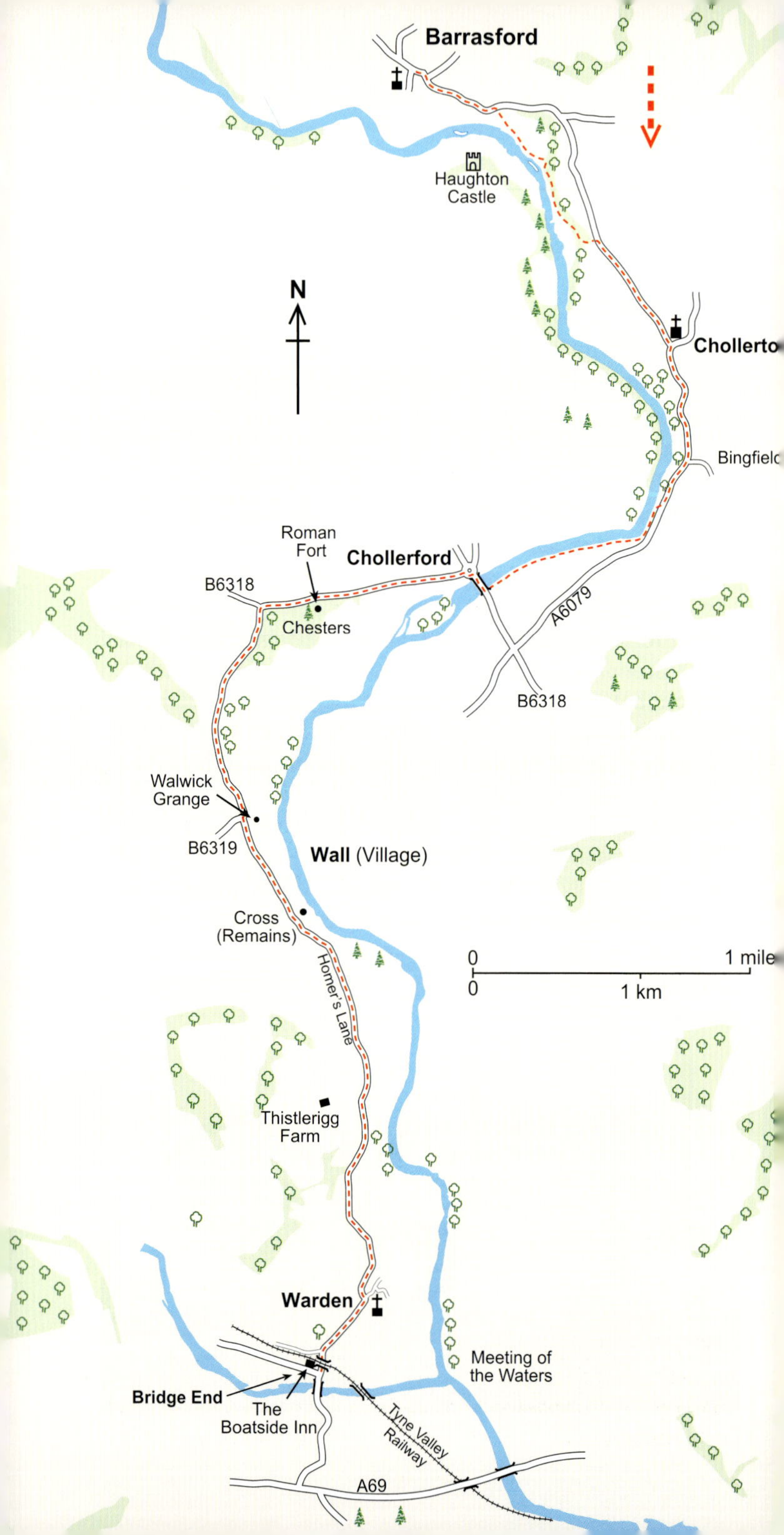

Barrasford
Haughton Castle
N
Chollerto
Bingfielc
Roman Fort
Chollerford
B6318
Chesters
A6079
B6318
Walwick Grange
B6319
Wall (Village)
Cross (Remains)
Homer's Lane
0
1 mile
0
1 km
Thistlerigg Farm
Warden
Meeting of the Waters
Bridge End
The Boatside Inn
Tyne Valley Railway
A69

STAGE 4
Barrasford to Warden
7 miles (11.3 km)

The walk continues down the North Tyne Valley as the river makes the final stage of its journey to its confluence with the River South Tyne. Soon you are high above the river which becomes visible from time to time through the tree-covered bankside. The river disappears totally from view as the trail follows a quiet road to the hamlet of Chollerton with its interesting church. You join a busier road before being rewarded with a delightful riverside section that leads to the only river crossing on this stage, the elegant bridge at Chollerford. This is now Hadrian's Wall territory and you pass the Roman Fort at Chesters.

The last section leads along a very quiet country lane for 2½ miles. It climbs steadily enabling you to appreciate the nature of the valley before descending to the parish area of Warden with its fine church and The Boatside Inn. Here you are within a short distance of the meeting of the waters of both the North and South Tyne and the beginning of the journey of the River Tyne itself to the sea. With this stage being relatively short you may wish to combine it with a further stage or make your way to the source of the South Tyne. Conveniently, Hexham with train, bus and taxi links is only 2½ miles further ahead.

Entry/exit points	**Barrasford (GR916734); Chollerford 3 miles (4.8km); Bridge End, Warden 7 miles (11.3km)**
Map	**OS Explorer OL43 Hadrian's Wall**
Refreshments	**Village shop and hotel in Barrasford; tea room and hotel at Chollerford; inn at Warden**

The walk

From the bus shelter at Barrasford, continue along the minor road past the Barrasford Arms. To your right you may catch a glimpse of Haughton Castle (dating from the 14th century, privately owned with holiday accommodation). The road is usually quiet, however, you can make use of the verge on the left-hand side as far as Hatchery House and then cross to the verge on the right-hand side of the road. After a few hundred yards you reach a bridge over the Swin Burn. Ignore the temptation to follow the fingerpost in the direction 'To Riverbank only', (this, in fact, leads to the landing stage of the former rope and pulley ferry to Haughton Castle) and, instead, a few paces after the bridge, turn right in the direction 'Chollerton 1¼'.

Go over the stile and bear immediately left on the path which climbs gradually until you are rewarded with views of the North Tyne as it is joined by the burn. Here the broad river appears to be rushing eagerly to its much more important meeting with the South Tyne a few miles ahead.

The path makes its way to a broad access track. Bear right along the track towards a metal gate behind which stands a rather substantial and forbidding-looking building. This is in fact a Northumbrian Water pumping station that transfers water from the river to West Hallington reservoir. However, fear not

Pumping station

that your route is blocked, as on your left you will find a little gate that leads on to a narrow path with a beech hedge on your right. You are soon at a stile.

Cross the stile and turn immediately left to follow the path as it climbs very steeply through the trees. You may need to be careful with your footing in wet weather. At the top of the rise turn right. Carry on between the trees along the top of the bankside. Even if the river is no longer visible you may still hear that it is close at hand. You cross a waymarked stile. The path descends to a small waymark post on your right. From here you may get your last glimpse of the river for a while. Parts of the path may be overgrown in summer and quite boggy after rainy periods so you may need to navigate your way carefully. After about 40yds, bear left to follow the path in the direction of the tree-line. Continue for about 200yds, passing a solitary hawthorn bush on your right, until you spot (at times with difficulty) a waymarked stile under the tree-line.

Once over the stile, follow the woodland path, with a tiny stream on your right, as it rises again very steeply and potentially slippery. At the top, you pass through an old gateway and then drop down into a narrow ditch. Hard though it is to imagine, this was once part of the Border Counties Railway! Bear right, then, ignoring a faint path off to the left towards a waymarked gate, follow the clear (permissive) path which rises to exit at a clearing, back onto the minor road on which you started.

Turn right. You now need to follow the road for about ½ mile. Although you can no longer see the river, at least you are moving in the same direction, and there are one or two things to catch the eye. You pass The Old Church where, somewhat discordantly, the roof is now lined with solar panels. Ahead to the left, you should see the base of a windmill at Chollerton. You pass The Vicarage before arriving at a junction with a more major road. Here you find the Church of St Giles at **Chollerton** on one side, and an imposing war memorial on the other side.

Proceed ahead towards Chollerford on a more main road, the A6079. You need to stay on this busier section for about two-thirds of a mile. Again due caution needs to be exercised. For most of the way there is a narrow verge as an escape route and it may be advisable to use the left-hand side verge as the road descends to a sharp bend and goes under the substantial old railway bridge (1858).

Chollerton

There has been a church on this site possibly since the 12th century and there is a gravestone of that era within the porch wall as well as some stone work believed to have come from the Roman Camp at Chesters which you will pass later. A Roman altar just inside the door serves as a font. You may find the church open and if so it is well worth a visit. However, passers-by may well wonder at the space-craft-looking addition to the tower! The quaint building beside the gate was in fact once the stable and hearse quarters for the church. Inspection of the war memorial indicates the high level of local involvement in two World Wars with an interesting range of regiments.

St Giles, Chollerton

After the bridge, a stream accompanies you on the left and you cross this before encountering the minor road to Bingfield coming in from your left. A straight stretch of road follows. You need to look out for a public footpath sign 'Chollerford 1' at a pull-in spot on the right-hand verge.

Leave the road and go down the stone steps to follow the path close to the high stone wall. At last the river returns into view on your right. The path again may be muddy in places but there is some helpful duck-boarding, if only it didn't end so abruptly! However, you soon find yourself walking along a field edge for quite some distance on a pleasant riverside path.

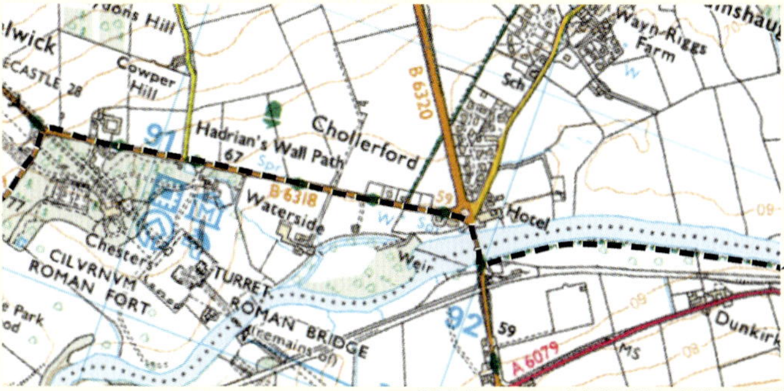

As you near the end of the field, on the other side of the river, you may see the George Hotel, in earlier times probably an 18th century coaching inn. Lord Baden-Powell, founder of the Scout Movement, was among the hotel's distinguished guests and it was here that he wrote part of *Scouting for Boys*, published in 1908.

You cross a stile and then stone steps take you up to Chollerford Bridge. The current bridge dates from 1785 when it replaced its medieval predecessor which was

Chollerford Bridge *(Photograph: Graeme Peacock)*

destroyed in the great flood of 1771. A convenient pavement leads you across the bridge, but do stop to admire the fine river views. Once over the river, you'll need to cross over to the other side of the road at the traffic lights that serve the one-way traffic system. Continue past (or visit) the Riverside Tea Room then cross over to the pavement on the right-hand side of the road.

Now walk alongside the B6318. This stretch of the trail is part of the Hadrian's Wall Path. The road is also known locally as the Military Road as it was originally built to facilitate troop movements after the 1745 Jacobite Rebellion. On your left, before long, you will see the entrance to the Roman Fort of Chesters.

Chesters

The fort built shortly after the Wall itself, probably about AD123, is run by English Heritage and is said to be "the best preserved example of a Roman cavalry fort in Britain". Here there are remains of the garrison camp, a museum, a tearoom (summer only) and a shop. There is also evidence nearby of two versions of Roman stone bridges across the North Tyne. If time permits a visit is recommended.

The grounds of the Chesters Estate also contain a substantial dwelling, not visible from the road, built in the late 18th century. John Clayton, who was to become like his father, Town Clerk of Newcastle, was brought up here and perhaps not surprisingly, as a noted antiquarian, he did a lot to preserve the Roman Wall.

Chesters Stud Farm (*Photograph: Richard Page*)

As you proceed further, on your right, you pass the impressive-looking former Chesters Stables/Stud Farm and the adjacent Butlers Cottage. Just before the road bears right, cross over with care to go down the B6319 towards your next destination signposted 'Warden 3'. You pass the attractive Gardeners Cottage on your right. There is no pavement from here onwards and, although the route ahead is generally very quiet, the usual care needs to be taken. At a junction where the B6319 bears right, you need to turn left, to follow the sign 'Warden 2¼'.

The minor road, known as Homer's Lane, passes traditional farm properties at Walwick Grange. It then undulates and zig-zags towards your current destination. On the left, you will come across a conveniently positioned bench and the remains of an ancient stone

Base of an ancient cross

cross. From this vantage point you may be able to see the river below or at least trace its tree-lined route along the steep North Tyne Valley. The aptly-named village of Wall lies on the other side of the valley. The narrow lane climbs steadily. Across the valley, see if you can spot, a maroon railway carriage at the site of the former Wall Station (closed 1955) on the dismantled Border Counties Railway.

After a long slow climb you pass the entrance to Thistlerigg and High Warden Farms. Now you can enjoy the descent into Low Warden. As the road levels off, it reaches an access road on the left where you will

St Michael and All Angels Church, Warden

catch sight of the capped tower of St Michael and All Angels Church.

It's worth taking a few extra strides to get a closer look at this church which has stood here in one form and other for over 1,300 years. The church noticeboard next to the attractive lychgate provides details of some of the key features. Near the main door stands an early 7th century stone cross moved here in 1957 and somewhat reminiscent of the remains of the stone base you passed earlier.

The road bears right and continues beneath a railway bridge, this time, one which carries traffic on the Newcastle to Carlisle Tyne Valley Line. Around the next corner is The Boatside Inn at Warden where your path converges with the route from the source of the South Tyne. The confluence of the two rivers awaits you a short way ahead but for now at the aptly named Bridge End you have completed this stage of the Daft as a Brush Cancer Patient Care Walk and with it the North Tyne section of the trail.

Meeting place

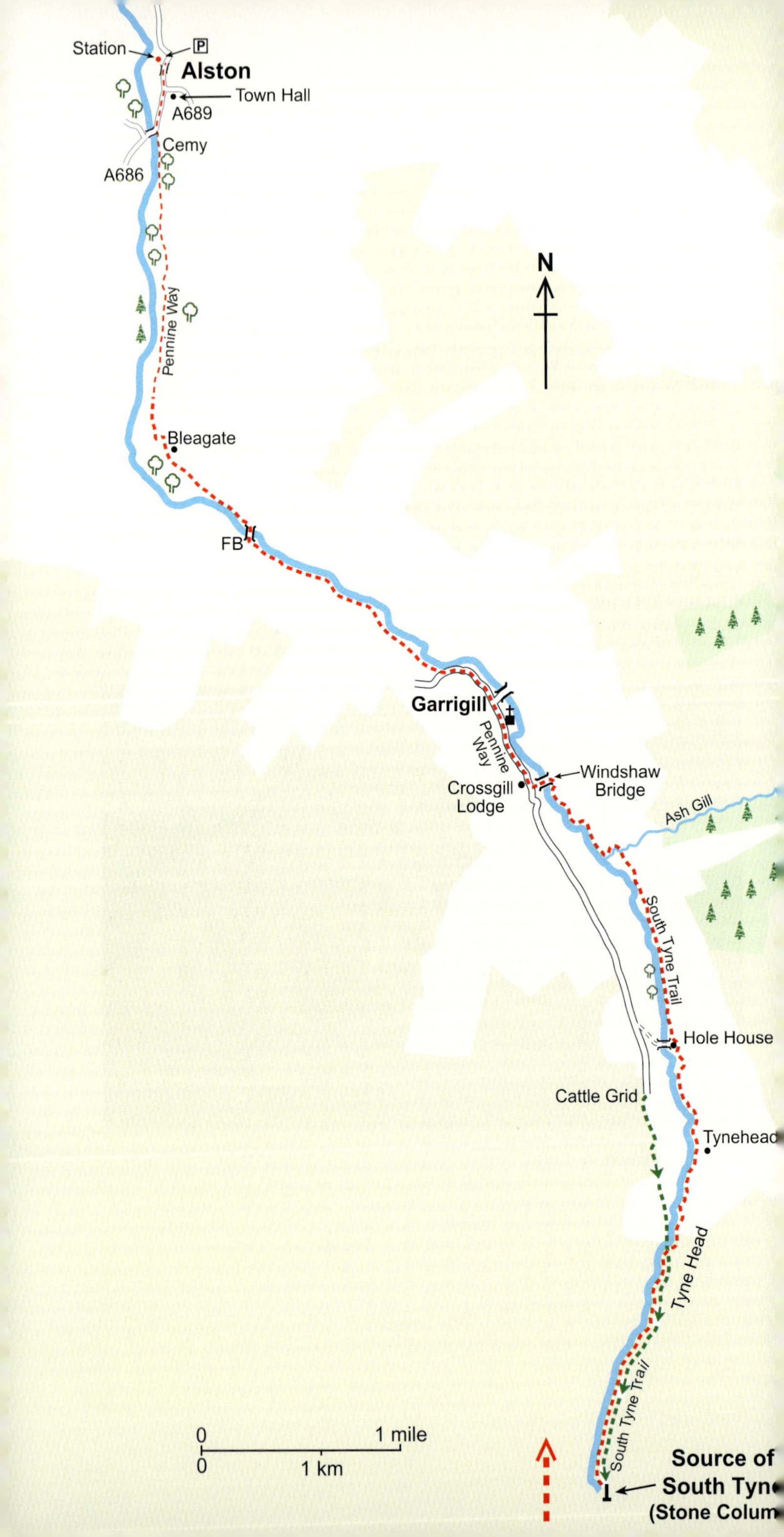

Station
P
Alston
Town Hall
A689
Cemy
A686
Pennine Way
N
Bleagate
FB
Garrigill
Pennine Way
Windshaw Bridge
Crossgill Lodge
Ash Gill
South Tyne Trail
Hole House
Cattle Grid
Tynehead
Tyne Head
South Tyne Trail
0
1 mile
0
1 km
Source of
South Tyne
(Stone Colum

STAGE 5

Source of the South Tyne to Alston

9¾ miles (15.7 km)

Before you reach the source you are faced with a 2 mile walk. Hence the total distance you will need to cover to complete this stage is 11¾ miles. Your starting point is from a gateway with a cattle grid, shortly after Hill House, at the end of the minor road from Garrigill. Beyond the gateway is a bridleway with no public vehicular access. So, boots on and away you go along the narrow track! After about ¾ mile you come to a set of fingerposts near a barn. A further 1¼ miles brings you to the sculpture which marks the source of the South Tyne. It is interesting to note that here in the North Pennine Hills, you are also not far from the sources of the two other great rivers of North East England, the Tees and the Wear.

From the source the trail follows the well-waymarked South Tyne Trail through Garrigill and on to Alston. After leaving the stony access track, the first ¾ mile is over rough moorland but thereafter you are on green paths. There are only two short climbs but there are a considerable number of stiles to cross, some of which are quite high! Although the waymarking is good, you will find that the distinctive South Tyne Trail signs are not so evident where there is existing public footpath or Pennine Way signage. You will be walking in an Area of Outstanding Natural Beauty (AONB), so expect some stunning views. You should enjoy seeing the river in its many different moods - from a tinkling trickle to a majestic wideness, passing waterfalls and deep ravines along the way. *The South Tyne Trail*

Entry/exit points	**Gateway/cattle grid at the end of the minor road from Garrigill (GR757384) ; Garrigill 5 miles (8km); Alston 9¾ miles (15.7km)**
Map	**OS Explorer OL31 North Pennines**
Refreshments	**Village shop in Garrigill, pubs and cafés in Alston**

leaflet, published by the East Cumbria Countryside project and available from Alston TIC, provides interesting background information about the route. There are fourteen river crossings on this stage of the route, although you will not encounter them all!

The walk

The source of the River South Tyne (GR753352) is marked by a sculpture by Gilbert Ward (2002). A few yards behind the sculpture, the infant South Tyne emerges, gurgling, from beneath a rock. You may wish to follow the sculptor's intention and look from the road through the slit to appreciate the beginnings of the river's development.

Source of South Tyne
(Photograph: Graeme Peacock)

Just at the right of the sculpture, the culvert taking the tiny rivulet under the road is the first of this stage's river crossings. Now head back down the access track to the fingerposts you passed earlier. On the way, it is fascinating to observe how the tiny rivulet on your left, fed by numerous tributaries, soon becomes a broader stream. Carry on as you pass a bridge on your left (the second river crossing on this stage). You are walking through an area rich in a variety of minerals, many of which were extracted in former times by the **South Tyne Mining Industry**. You will come across evidence, for example, in the form of spoil heaps, from these activities.

After 1¼ miles you reach the fingerposts you passed on the way to the source. Looking a few paces further ahead, you'll see that the river goes under a bridge (third crossing but from now onwards you'll have to note the crossings yourself!). However, before that point, you need to bear right at the barn and follow the direction indicated for the South Tyne Trail and Garrigill. The waymarking is good,

South Tyne Mining Industry

Much of the North Pennine fells area is rich in mineral deposits and mining has been a feature since Roman times, with evidence of mining activity in Cumbria, Durham and Northumberland. Over the centuries, different methods have been used and different minerals have been mined. Around Alston, silver deposits were exploited in the 13th century. Mining experienced a rapid growth from the early 18th century; the richness of lead deposits proved particularly attractive. For a time, the London Lead Company, a Quaker establishment, was one of the principal participants and led the way in introducing enlightened practices.

Mining gradually declined from the mid-19th century and had all but died out by the 1950s. One of Alston's lesser known claims to fame is that alstonite was named after it. However, the mineral is probably too rare to be of commercial use but does find favour with collectors. For more detail about local geology, an English Nature leaflet *Tynehead Geological Trail* describes a 2 mile walk, part of which you will be covering, which "will introduce many of the rocks that give the landscape of the North Pennines its unique character".

The river develops *(Photograph: Graeme Peacock)*

although the path is indistinct in parts.

Climb in the direction indicated, keeping to the right of the large barn, to the next waymark. Bear in mind that you are following the river on your left, although initially you are taken slightly away so as to avoid a difficult section. Near the beginning, the waymarks appear at regular, fairly short intervals. Soon the path descends and you walk to the foot of a wall ahead where there is another waymark. You come to a stile, the first of many on this stage of the trail. You will meet a variety of stile styles, some of which need very careful negotiation (at least that's what your septuagenarian authors found!).

Dorthgill Falls
(Photograph: Richard Page)

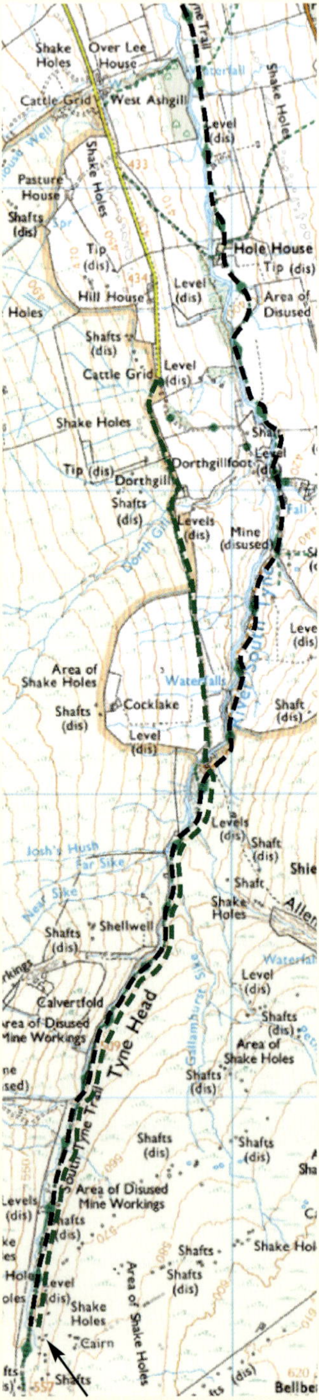

You arrive at the dramatic Dorthgill Falls; with its steep sides overlooked by a backdrop of pine trees it makes a delightful picture. Even if you are in a hurry, do pause to admire the view – walking by and looking down is not recommended!

Continue ahead over rough ground to a stile. Gradually you descend towards a farmhouse passing some ruined buildings before reaching a waymarked gate below the house (Tynehead). Before moving on, if you are a river crossings 'collector', you should be able to spot a footbridge over the South Tyne, a little over to your left.

Go through the gate, turn right and cross the tiny bridge over the Clargill Burn. At the fingerpost, follow the direction indicated for the South Tyne Trail and Garrigill and go over the gated stile. Carry on until you meet a wall and a waymark directs you to bear right, away from the river. After some 60yds go over the waymarked stile next to a gate and walk ahead to go through another gate. Carry on towards the farm buildings of Hole House. Go through another gate and bear right to a further gate at the corner of the barn. Turn left to exit the farmyard through yet another gate. (There is a bridge over the river beyond the farm. Anyone daunted by the prospect of more stiles could leave the trail here and retrace their steps along the road to Garrigill thus avoiding some of the most awkward stiles).

Cross the farm road and go over a narrow awkward stile. Now continue ahead with the river close by and go over a further stile. Continue ahead and be prepared for another awkward stile with quite a drop on the other side and a stream to negotiate. You pass through a young plantation and the path becomes a little more defined taking you past the first of three gates.

Eventually the path climbs away from the river towards a farmhouse. Turn left at the waymark post, cross a stile and continue ahead until you reach a footbridge over the Ash Gill. A fingerpost invites a short diversion to Ashgill Force, where it is worth the five minute stroll to a bridge from which you can view the upper fall. You may even encounter some brave gorge walkers near here!

However, to continue on the South Tyne Trail, you need to turn left and follow the tributary a short way to its confluence with the South Tyne. Go over the stile and now follow the tree-lined riverside path. You come to a point where the river cuts through a deep ravine. In winter

Ashgill Force (Photograph: Graeme Peacock)

months, when the banks are bare of vegetation, you can appreciate their depth and steepness.

Follow the river to reach a set of waymarks inviting you to cross a bridge. Do not cross this bridge but carry straight on. You come to a stone bridge which you do cross. This is Windshaw Bridge which takes you high above the South Tyne and leads to a short path which meets a minor road at Crossgill Lodge. Turn right and walk along the minor road. After a gradual climb the road descends quite steeply.

Just after the sign indicating your arrival in **Garrigill**, the Pennine Way, which you will follow all the way to Alston, joins the road from the left. Continue ahead past St John's Church to the village green. You may wish to pause here after your 5 mile walk from the source of the South Tyne. The end of this stage at Alston Station now lies a further 4¾ miles ahead.

To continue to Alston, carry on along the road with the village green on your right. At the end of the village you pass a white house, the 'Old School', the former girls' school of 1850, now a private dwelling. The road bears

Joining the Pennine Way at Garrigill

Garrigill

Garrigill is a small, attractive Cumbrian village. Formerly it was an important centre of the local lead mining industry with a population of up to 1000. Its population now is around 200. It is a useful stopping off place for cyclists on the Sea to Sea (C2C) Cycle Route and the long-distance Pennine Way walk passes through the village. The village green, the George and Dragon pub (sadly closed at the time of writing), the Post Office (which acts as a traditional village store) and St John's Church all contribute to the village atmosphere.

The present building of the Church of St John dates from the 18th century but has been subject to lots of restoration since then. The Christian presence on this site dates back to at least 1215. Interestingly, although it is located in Cumbria, the church lies within the ecclesiastical Diocese of Newcastle upon Tyne.

left and ascends. On your right, you pass a couple of fingerposts to Beldy Chapel (former Wesleyan Chapel), and you see a footbridge over the river, before reaching a fingerpost indicating 'Pennine Way; South Tyne Trail; Alston 3¾'. Go onto the path and proceed ahead. Soon you pass an eclectic collection of equipment and some small spoil heaps.

You cross a gated stile and then follow the path as it climbs quite steeply. You are now on a much more trodden path which will eventually lead you all the way to Alston, thanks to the Pennine Way. At the top of the rise you are rewarded with fine views across the river where you see a patchwork of stone walls separating the fields and woodlands. Then, as you look ahead, you can see the rolling hills of the North Pennines beckoning you forward. You soon

Slate river bed (*Photograph: Graeme Peacock*)

descend to follow a peaceful riverside path alongside the, now wide, South Tyne. You cross a series of stiles as you keep close to the river and ignore any paths off to the left.

You will notice plenty of evidence of flat slate river bed where the water flows smoothly before cascading over rockier sections. Lovers of wild flowers will be delighted to spot numerous species according to season such as: violets, celandine, speedwell, butterbur, wood-sorrel and stitchworts.

In just over 1½ miles you reach a fine footbridge. Cross the narrow bridge and turn left. Continue ahead

A fine foot bridge

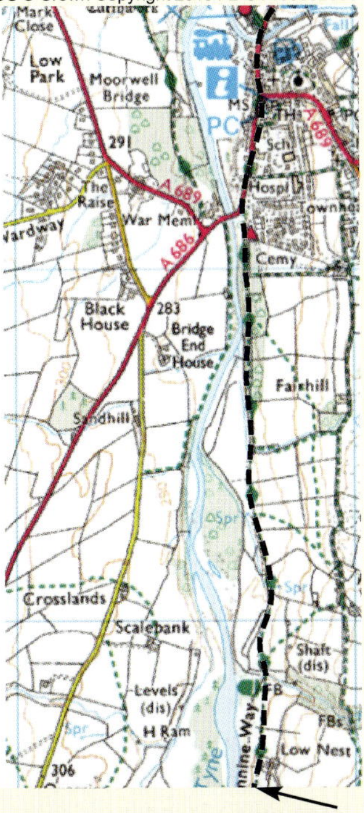

with the river on your left. After you pass through a wide gap in a stone wall, bear immediately right at a Pennine Way sign. Now follow the path close to the stone wall on your right as you move away from the river. The path leads to a further Pennine Way fingerpost some 50yds from the end of the field. Here you climb steeply to go over a stile in the top right-hand corner. Continue to climb to another fingerpost beside which there is a convenient stone bench where you can rest and enjoy the sound, if not always the sight, of the river.

Walk to the wall ahead, bear left, then right, to go through the gap in the wall. Now proceed diagonally left uphill to go over a gated stile in the wall. Continue climbing before the path descends with a wall on your right towards some farm buildings at Bleagate. Exit onto the road, turn left past the house and bear right towards the gate. Cross the stile next to the gate and turn right. Now proceed ahead along the right-hand boundary to go over a stile and then through gaps in the wall over three fields. After another stile you find a stone wall on your left. After about 50yds bear left at a waymark post to go through a gap in the wall. Continue with the wall and a copse of trees on your right, then, at the waymark, cross to the other side of the wall and proceed once more ahead.

Follow the clear path over stiles and gaps in walls passing the occasional property. Carry on until you cross a footbridge. Continue ahead over further stiles. You pass a memorial stone bench on your left before going through a small wooden gate and onto the pleasant tree-lined path. The river gradually appears below and eventually you pass Alston Cemetery and then Alston Youth Hostel. On your left is The Firs Stone, describing the formation of a local woodland walk. You exit onto an access road. Turn left and walk a short distance to join a road. Turn left again down the pavement to meet the main A686. (A further river crossing in the form of a road bridge lies to the left). However, turn right, cross the road when convenient, and continue ahead alongside the A686 (Station Road) through **Alston**. Should you wish to visit the Town Hall (Tourist Information Centre) and/or the Market Cross, you need to turn right at the major junction (A689). Otherwise continue a short distance until you reach the railway station on your left. Here is the end of this stage of the Daft as a Brush Cancer Patient Care Walk.

Alston

Alston is situated in the upper South Tyne Valley, within the North Pennines Area of Outstanding Natural Beauty (AONB). It is a pleasant little town noted for its cobbled streets, late 17th and early 18th century buildings, the Market Cross and an early 19th century church. It can no longer claim to be the highest market town in England (it is many years since a market was held here) but its altitude of 1000 feet (304m), together with its remote setting, makes it an appropriate stopping place for visitors.

Market Cross, Alston (*Photograph: Graeme Peacock*)

The fells around the town are rich in mineral deposits and mining was a significant part of the local economy for many years. Now, sheep farming, some high-tech development and tourism are important features. Tourism makes use of aspects of mining history and many farmers have diversified, for example, in the provision of bed and breakfast accommodation. Today's visitors to this attractive small town include walkers on the long-distance Pennine Way and cyclists on the C2C (Sea to Sea Cycle Route). The well-stocked Tourist Information Centre is located in the Town Hall.

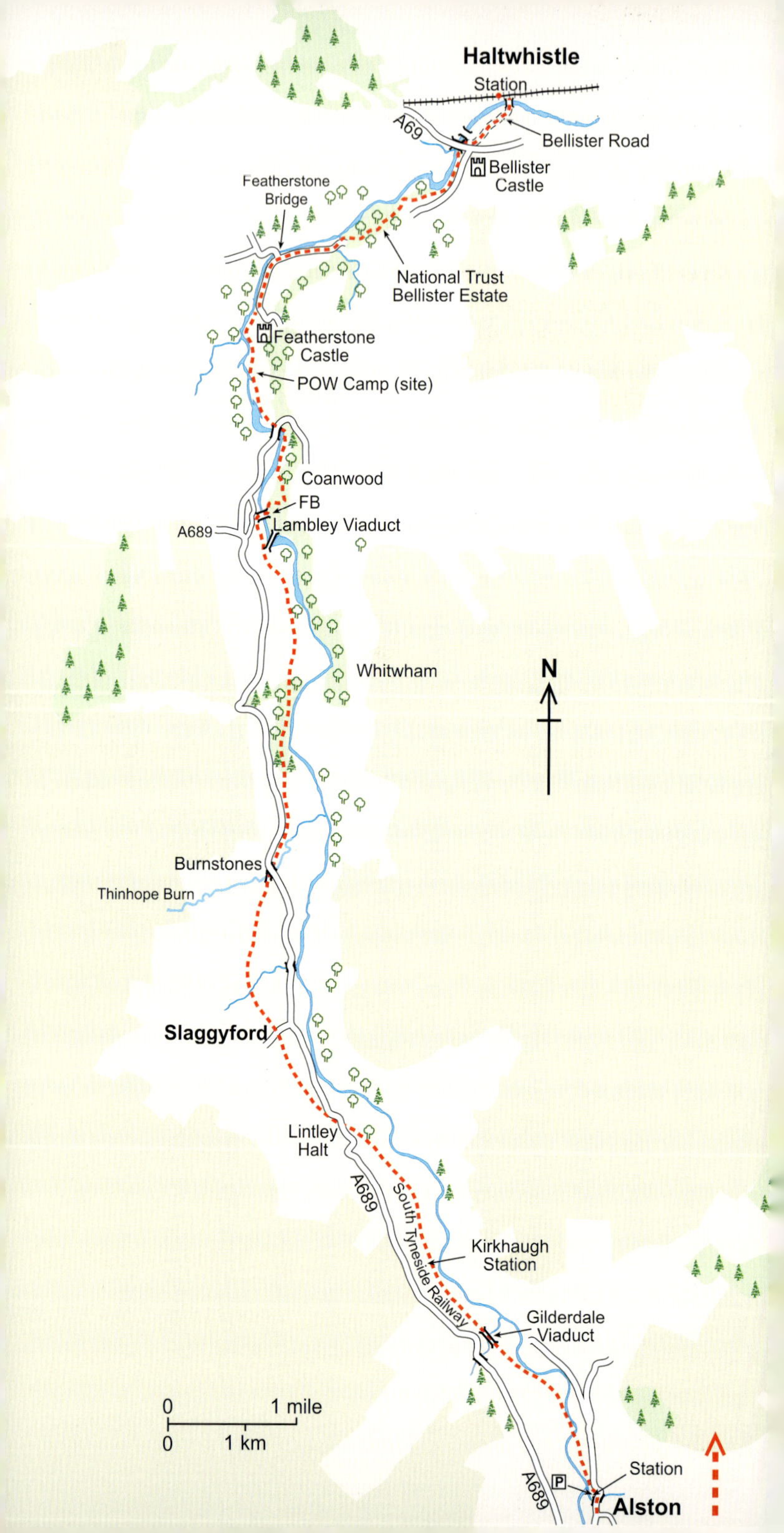
Haltwhistle
Station
A69
Bellister Road
Bellister Castle
Featherstone Bridge
National Trust Bellister Estate
Featherstone Castle
POW Camp (site)
Coanwood
FB
Lambley Viaduct
A689
Whitwham
N
Burnstones
Thinhope Burn
Slaggyford
Lintley Halt
A689
South Tyneside Railway
Kirkhaugh Station
Gilderdale Viaduct
0
1 mile
0
1 km
A689
P
Station
Alston

STAGE 6
Alston to Haltwhistle

13¾ miles (22.1 km)

This stage starts from the railway station in the Cumbrian market town of Alston. 'The Hub' local history museum is located in the former goods shed. Initially, we follow the **South Tynedale Railway**, a preserved 3½ mile section of the original Haltwhistle to Alston line. For most of the route you are walking by or near to the South Tyne. You are diverted away from the river a few times but overall you can enjoy a rich mix of riverside, woodland and field paths, with just a mile section on a quiet country lane. Interesting man-made features include numerous railway bridges, several viaducts, two castles and the remains of a former prisoner of war camp. For many people the highlight is the opportunity to walk along the dizzy height of the Lambley Viaduct, although this can be avoided if you are not too keen on walking tall! This is certainly the most spectacular of the fourteen river crossings on this stretch of the river, ten of which you will probably see. The walk is generally on the level with the only notable steep descents and ascents at Lambley and the Bellister Estate.

Entry/exit points	Alston (GR716462), Slaggyford 4½ miles (7.2km); Coanwood Station car park 9½ miles (15.3km); Haltwhistle 13¾ miles (22.1km)
Maps	OS Explorer OL31 North Pennines; OS Explorer OL43 Hadrian's Wall
Refreshments	Several cafés and pubs in Alston and Haltwhistle

South Tynedale Railway

The Newcastle and Gateshead Railway Company, which had run a service between Carlisle and Newcastle since 1839, opened its first branch line, from Haltwhistle to Alston, in 1851-2. This branch line, which carried freight and passengers,

Alston Station (*Photograph: Graeme Peacock*)

ran until 1976. Government approval for its closure had been passed in 1973. In that year a group of enthusiasts formed the South Tynedale Railway Preservation Society, with the objective of preserving the line. This proved to be impossible, hence the adoption by the Society of a new objective: building a narrow gauge tourist railway to be run mainly by volunteers.

To date, 3½ miles of track have been completed from Alston to Lintley. The award in 2014 of a Heritage Lottery Grant will facilitate plans which include extending the line by another 1½ miles to Slaggyford, as well as renovating an engine to its former glory. During the summer season the line provides an exciting journey for tourists to enjoy.

The walk

From Alston Station, cross the railway line and turn right. An information panel gives details of the South Tyne Trail and a fingerpost points the way to Slaggyford and Coanwood. Now proceed ahead along the permissive path. The building on the right is the carriage workshop.

You pass a plaque about a nature trail project. As you make your way along the line, you will find information panels about, among other things, the geology and bird life of the area. You may even spot some animals (albeit some carved ones!)

Cross the line as indicated. You go over a bridge which takes you and the railway across the South Tyne (first crossing on this stage). A sign invites you to climb to an attractive picnic site, although it may be a little too soon in your case. You are going to pass under a number of bridges, most of which appear to serve as links between farm fields and you will also cross several viaducts. The work involved in constructing these 19th century structures has to be admired.

After about 1½ miles you walk across the Gilderdale Viaduct which carries the railway over the burn of that name. It is particularly significant in that mid-way across you leave Cumbria and enter Northumberland.

Adjacent to the next nature panel, on the right, you might spot a fox! You arrive at the platform of the former Kirkhaugh Station, now a stopping place for the South Tynedale trains. Carry straight on, passing a fingerpost on the right

OS © Crown Copyright 2015 FL-GV100032058

Along the line

indicating 'Isaac's Tea Trail', which "follows the footsteps of the legendary tea seller Isaac Holden".

Continue to "your next station stop", as they say on mainline trains. This is Lintley Halt, currently the line's terminus, where train passengers (and walkers!) can relax at the picnic tables provided. However, the current plan is to extend the line for a further 1½ miles from here to Slaggyford.

The surfaced path becomes a grassy track and soon you go under a bridge. The track can become muddy. You go under another bridge, immediately after which, if the track is boggy, following local custom and practice, you can bear right up the bankside on your right. You can now carry on walking alongside

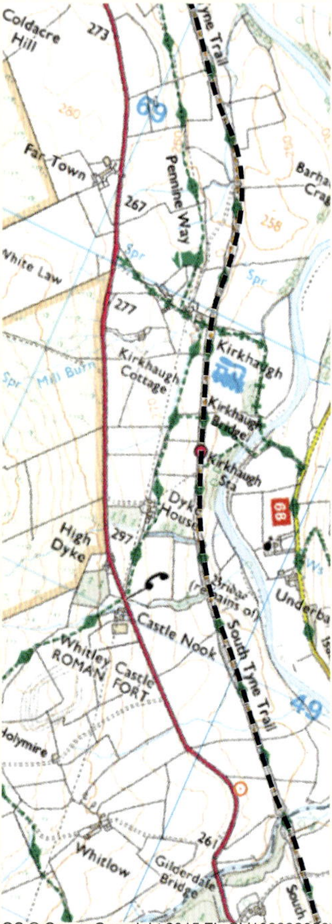

Slaggford Station

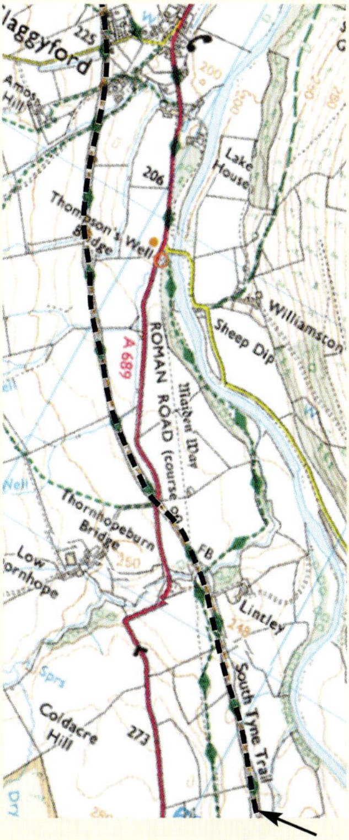

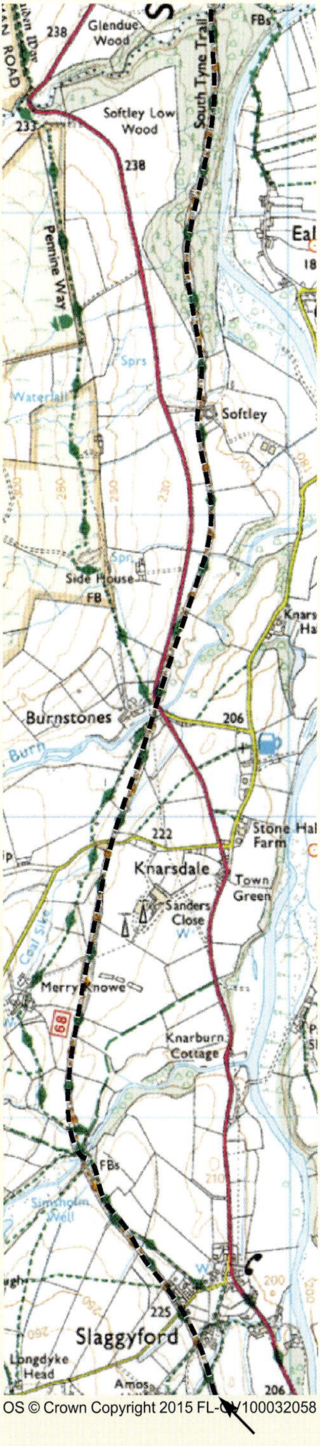

the fence on your right so as to avoid the boggy section below. You can then drop down to the lower level and continue to Slaggyford where you cross a road. A panel gives information about local access land. The Preservation Society's extension plans include renovation of the station building and the platform, which presently sports a grassy surface.

Proceed ahead, between the platform and the former station house. The path takes you along a tree-lined avenue for some distance after which you can enjoy views of the open country with a backdrop of hills on both sides.

Eventually you arrive at the Burnstones Viaduct which takes the railway across the Thinhope Burn and over the main A689 Alston to Brampton road. To the left is Burnstones and an entrance to the Knarsdale Estates. If you look over the wall on your right, you will see a road bridge, the Kirkstyle Inn and, a little further away, St Jude's Church (1833). In a short distance, at a clearing, you pass an encouraging sign 'Lambley Viaduct 2½'.

You walk through a delightful wooded area after which you come across a notice near Whitwham Farm with pictures of the different birds which inhabit this area. Although these do not include anything rare enough to produce an itching in the twitching fraternity, we lesser mortals will be thrilled if we spot them. A notice lets you know that you are walking through the Knarsdale Estates. A bench provides the opportunity for a short rest.

You cross an access road by some former railway cottages and are rewarded with your first view of the magnificent **Lambley Viaduct**. You come to a fingerpost indicating that you are 5

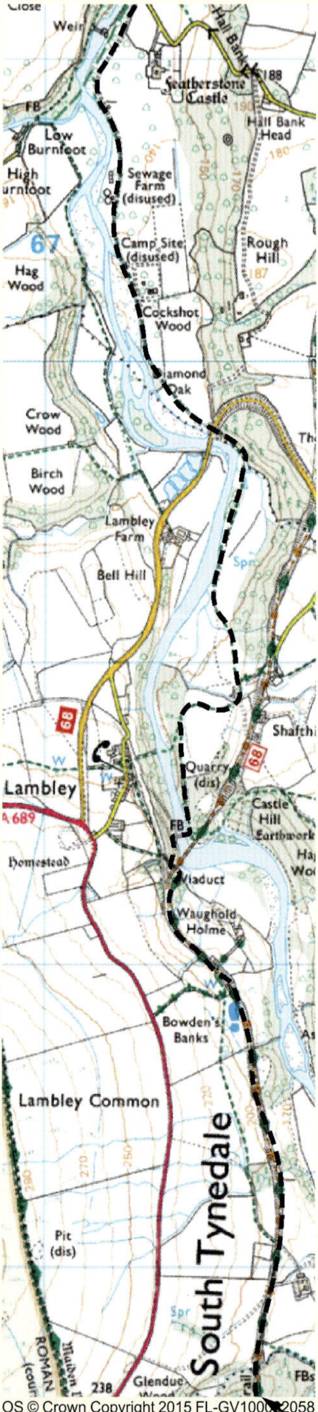

miles from Haltwhistle and ¼ mile from the Lambley Viaduct itself.

Now you have to leave the former railway track, as the house ahead is privately owned and there is no access to the beginning of the viaduct. Instead, you need to turn right and descend steeply via the steps. Above the garden, on your left, you can see what was Lambley Station. You go under the towering viaduct then climb steeply up the steps to arrive at a set of fingerposts.

Lambley Viaduct

The Alston to Haltwhistle branch of the Carlisle to Newcastle Railway operated from 1852 to 1976. Today we can still marvel at the Victorian builders who had to construct nine viaducts in the line's short, 13-mile length. Six of these were over tributaries and three, at Alston, Lambley and Haltwhistle crossed the River South Tyne.

The impressive Lambley Viaduct carried the line over a steep-sided tree-lined valley by nine semi-circular arches each 56 feet (17m) wide, with its deck being some 110 feet (34m) above the river. Following the line's closure, the viaduct fell into disrepair. However, it was restored in 1991, including repointing with flexible lime mortar as used originally, by British Railways before their tenure came to an end. As for its future – watch this space!

If you wish to experience a walk along the top of the magnificent Victorian structure, you need to follow the instructions, shown below in brackets,

(Turn left and follow the direction for 'South Tyne Trail (North) via Lambley Viaduct'. Climb the steep steps to reach the former track on the top where you can amble along the permissive path, pausing to appreciate both the splendid views and the tremendous achievements of the Victorian builders. Here you have a choice. Either retrace your steps back to the signposts or carry on to the end of the viaduct. After about 600yds you pass through a gateway into a small open space 'Coanwood Station car park'. After a further 15yds you need to make sure to turn sharp left and go through a metal gate to follow the sign, 'Public Right of Way Lambley Footbridge'. Go down the broad track to an isolated property. Here, you rejoin the main route at (**A**) below.)

High and low crossings at Lambley
(Photograph: Graeme Peacock)

Otherwise, to continue on the main route, follow the signposted direction to 'South Tyne Footbridge, Coanwood ¾'. You descend, via steps, to a bend in the river, from where you have further excellent views of the viaduct. Walk to the footbridge and go across. Turn left and walk ahead via a metal gate/stile. Continue ahead on the faint path for a couple of hundred yards or thereabouts, then bear right to the waymarked post on the raised section of the field. Walk diagonally left up the field to the top corner where you join a track descending from the right. Bear left through a metal gate to cross a bridge over a stream and walk past the isolated property. The alternative route across the Lambley Viaduct rejoins the main route here (**A**).

The next section takes you along a very faint path where, usually, there are muddy bits. Walk to the right of the copse of trees and then gradually bear left towards the river. Proceed alongside the river. Keep to the right of the trees to pick up a vehicular track and climb up the track to exit at a road. Watch out for fast traffic, then cross the road, turn right and walk to the nearby fingerpost. Proceed in the direction indicated for 'Featherstone Footbridge 1¼ miles'.

You now follow the track which soon runs alongside the river. Be aware of the danger from erosion and in particular keep well clear of the edge of the exit road. Go to the left of the sad-looking remains of a former Second World War **Prisoner of War Camp**.

Prisoner of War Camp

Camp 18, as it was known, was one of the largest POW camps in the country. It was constructed in 1944 and initially housed US military personnel before they embarked for the Normandy invasion. For the next few months, it accommodated Italian prisoners of war. However, from 1945 to 1948 it became a prison camp for German officers and high-ranking civilians, who underwent what turned out to be a successful rehabilitation programme. An important contribution to the process was made by Captain Herbert Sulzbach.

After several hundred yards the path passes between two stone pillars – the remains of the original gates to the camp. After passing through the gateway, make sure to look back at the left-hand pillar where you will find a plaque that makes reference to the role of Captain Sulzbach. Continue ahead, passing **Featherstone Castle** on your right.

You reach a gateway which leads to a road. Do not attempt to go through the gate; instead, turn left and walk alongside the fence on your right for a short distance to

Featherstone Castle *(Photograph: Graeme Peacock)*

Featherstone Castle

The history of a manor house and later castle dates from the 11th century. The oldest ownership can be traced to the Featherstonehaugh family. They sold the castle in the early 17th century but bought it back in 1711. Subsequent owners made considerable changes, the last major work being a restoration and enlargement in the 1820s by the Hon. Thomas Wallace. Much of what you now see is the result of his work, together with the 14th century tower.

The castle has been used in a variety of ways, including as a boys prep school. It is privately owned but in the early 1960s was converted into a residential self-catering conference and activity centre. Like many Gothic-style castles, Featherstone is said to be haunted. This probably adds to its attraction for the eclectic set of visiting groups who enjoy its basic facilities.

meet another gate. Almost immediately on your left, you may see the pedestrian bridge that was largely destroyed in the flood of May 2013.

Go through the gate to join a road. Turn left to walk along this pleasant and normally quiet country lane for about a mile. You pass the splendid mid-19th century Featherstone Bridge on your left. Proceed ahead and, just after passing the Camping and Caravanning Club site on the left, you come to the National Trust Bellister Estate information

On route to Haltwhistle *(Photograph: Graeme Peacock)*

panel. This describes a permissive circular walk through the estate. You can now make use of the easterly section to take you to Haltwhistle. Care is needed in several places where the path is narrow and there is evidence of erosion. There are some steep inclines.

Go through the gate and follow the narrow path straight ahead. You can now enjoy a pleasant, undulating woodland walk, with some good views of the South Tyne below for much of the way. Ignore any paths off. This ancient woodland is a real treat for nature lovers with its abundant wild flowers. Look out too for the deer. You may be able to pause awhile on a bench or even at a picnic table.

Eventually, when you are high above the river, the path leads through a gate. Turn left and follow the fence for a short distance. Turn right at the waymark. The ground here is often muddy. Now climb straight ahead to go through a gate. Thereafter continue to enjoy the woodland. When you reach high ground where the path is fenced on both sides, you should be able to obtain a view of the river as it flows to the road bridge over the A69 with Haltwhistle beyond.

Eventually, you come to an inviting bench and a plaque inscribed with a poem *Nature's Magic*. Turn left at the junction of paths, walk downhill with a road nearby to your right and then descend via a series of steep steps to the riverside. Continue ahead on the pleasant path. After a 150yds or so, over to the right, you may be able to see the ruins of the 14th century Bellister Castle, which is attached to a 19th century mansion house.

Turn right to leave the riverside, at a power line, just before the bridge which carries the A69 Haltwhistle bypass over the river. Follow the stepped path to reach an access road. (Note that Stage 7 returns to this point from Haltwhistle. However, if you decide not to stop at Haltwhistle, turn right here and follow Stage 7 from (**A**).)

To proceed to Haltwhistle, turn left and go under the bridge. Continue ahead. You pass through a gate. Ignore the public bridleway on your left. Carry on for about a third of a mile, then turn left to cross a bridge over the South Tyne. Go under the railway bridge up Boat Lane and turn left at the road ahead. In a short distance, at a crossroads, turn right for the amenities of **Haltwhistle** or turn left into the station car park where you will find two information panels at the formal end of this stage of the Daft as a Brush Cancer Patient Care Walk.

Haltwhistle

Haltwhistle is a small, busy, pleasant Northumbrian town. Light industries are located away from the centre, which remains unspoilt. However, it is tourism which now provides the most substantial input into the local economy. The town itself has a Thursday market which dates back to the 13th century, as does its parish church, Holy Cross, which is rated as a fine and complete example of the period. Spring and autumn Walking Festivals were started in 2003 and have proved to be extremely popular. Proximity to Hadrian's Wall and Roman and other historic sites are added attractions for today's tourist.

Haltwhistle claims to be the centre of Britain. Town inhabitants are proud of this and, understandably, it features heavily in promoting the town. It is only fair to point out that other locations have been suggested as the centre but Haltwhistle's citizens will, no doubt, continue to defend their claim.

Haltwhistle Centre of Britain *(Photograph: Graeme Peacock)*

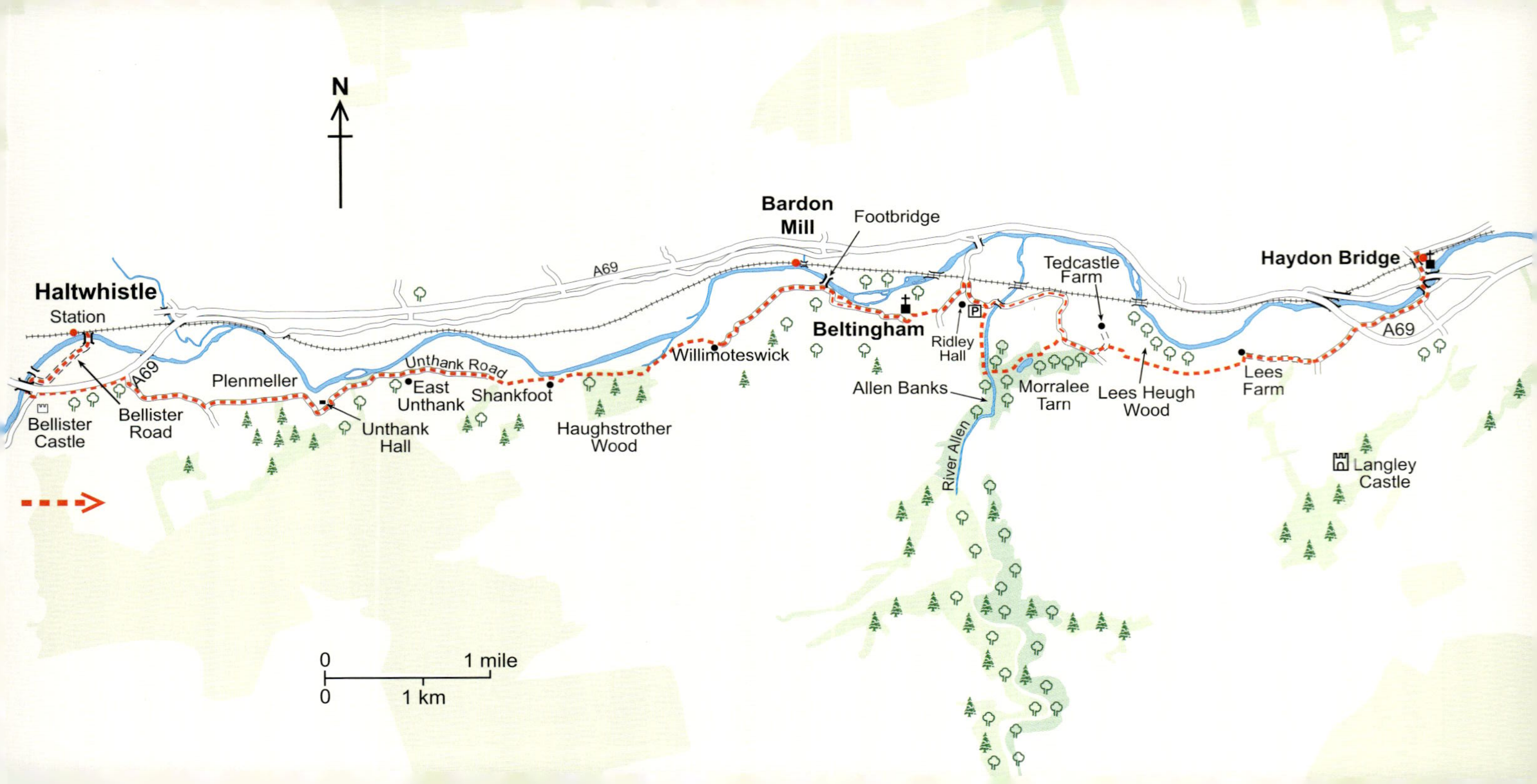
N
Haltwhistle
Station
Bellister Castle
Bellister Road
A69
Plenmeller
Unthank Road
East Unthank
Unthank Hall
Shankfoot
Haughstrother Wood
Willimoteswick
Bardon Mill
Footbridge
Beltingham
Ridley Hall
Allen Banks
River Allen
Morralee Tarn
Tedcastle Farm
Lees Heugh Wood
Lees Farm
Haydon Bridge
Langley Castle
0
1 mile
0
1 km

STAGE 7
Haltwhistle to Haydon Bridge
12 miles (19.3km)

Access to a riverside path on this stage of the trail, at the time of writing, is limited to only one short stretch. However, there are many fine views of the South Tyne as the walk takes you through attractive wooded areas as well as across open countryside. You pass a number of small farming communities and a variety of attractive properties. Interesting features on route include an impressive castle gatehouse, a charming old church associated with a 7th century northern saint, St Cuthbert, as well as a 20th century member of the Royal Family and a former stately hall. About two-thirds of the route is along very quiet minor roads. There are several climbs some of which are quite steep. The National Trust at Allen Banks offers you the opportunity to stroll alongside the River Allen, an important tributary of the South Tyne, and then climb through some ancient woodlands and past a delightful tarn. You follow part of a heritage trail associated with a noted local artist. There are nine river crossings, including four rail bridges, but you only cross the South Tyne when you reach Haydon Bridge.

Entry/exit points	**Haltwhistle (GR704638); Bardon Mill 6 miles (9.7km); Beltingham 7 miles (11.3km); National Trust car park at Allen Banks 8 miles (12.9km); Haydon Bridge 12 miles (19.3km)**
Map	**OS Explorer OL43 Hadrian's Wall**
Refreshments	**A selection of possibilities at both Haltwhistle, Bardon Mill and Haydon Bridge**

The walk

From Haltwhistle railway station, walk to the crossroads, with The Railway Inn just beyond, and turn right. (From Platform 2 you can access the trail directly by following the

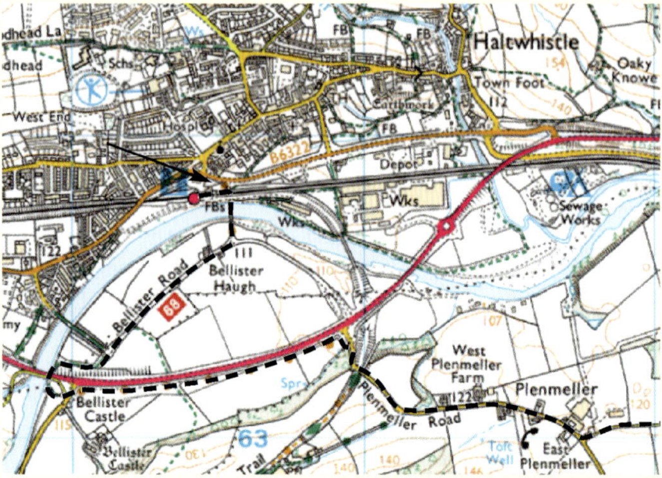

sign 'Way out avoiding footbridge'.) Proceed a short way before turning right to go under the railway line at Boat Lane. Continue ahead on the bridge over the South Tyne from where, to the left, you will see some of the fine arches of the now disused Haltwhistle Railway Viaduct (1851-1976). You arrive at a junction where you turn right. Walk along the access road (Bellister Road), go through a gate and pass under the busy A69. You arrived at this point previously on Stage 6 (**A**). Continue ahead on the access road to come to a gate next to a cattle grid and a Cycleway 68 sign. Cross over the road and go through a gateway. The ruins of Bellister Castle lie ahead.

Bellister Castle

However, you need to turn immediately left and proceed along the surfaced cycleway in the direction indicated by the Cycleway 68 sign. Carry on, walking parallel with the A69 on the left. Exit via a gate onto a road (Plenmeller Road). Turn right and continue along this minor road. You pass through pleasant farmland with the scattered and at times substantial dwellings of Plenmeller on either side of the road. At a junction, turn left to follow the sign 'Unthank – No through road'.

This road stretches almost straight ahead for about ¾ mile before bearing right and then left past some delightful cottages, the austere-looking Unthank Hall and the adjacent farm buildings. Ignore the public footpath ahead and instead follow the road as it descends to the left. You pass the remains of a walled garden. Eventually the river comes into view as you look across to Melkridge. The road bears left over a cattle grid just before East Unthank Farm.

Continuing ahead, you pass some barns and outbuildings at Shankfoot, where, at some white gateposts, the road bends sharply to the right. Climb between the farm buildings and turn left to cross a stone bridge and a cattle grid. Now keep straight ahead on the track, ignoring paths off, until a gate leads into Haughstrother Wood.

Proceed ahead along the forest track which may be churned and rutted depending on the weather and whether logging is taking place. At a junction keep straight ahead on the main track which climbs steadily, ignoring work access tracks. Eventually the track descends to exit from the woods at a gate. The river becomes visible ahead. In a short distance, bear right to join a metalled access track. Follow the track for about 150yds, go over a waymarked stile and

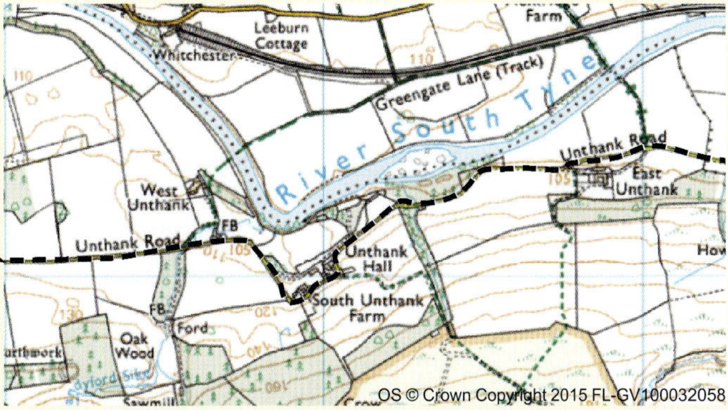

Through Haughstrother Wood

pass outbuildings and a cottage to join a further vehicular track. After a level section, the track climbs steadily up to the impressive castle gatehouse and farm of Willimoteswick.

A 16th century fortified manor house, it was the principal residence of the Ridley family and it is claimed to have been the birthplace of Bishop Nicholas Ridley who was martyred in 1555. The curious name is thought to be derived from either 'guillemot' or 'William'.

Turn left at the farm buildings to join a minor road and bear left down the road, passing Bridge Cottage. After about ¾ mile you reach a clearing on your left, behind which there is a footbridge over the South Tyne. Walk towards the footbridge but do not cross it unless you wish to go an extra ¼ mile to the village of Bardon Mill where you will find

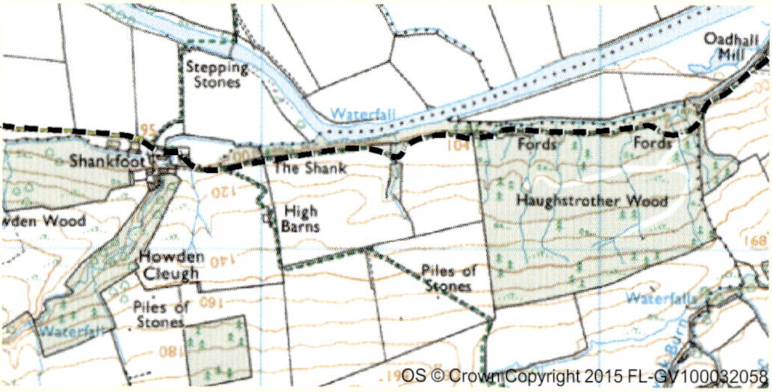

Climbing to Willimoteswick

Bardon Mill Pottery, Railway Station, the Village Shop and Tearoom, the Bowes Hotel and several B&Bs.

Instead, turn right at the green railings and bear left onto the narrow path which leads into a Wildlife Nature Reserve. (However, after heavy rain, this route may be impassable, in which case you need to proceed along the minor road you have just left.) The path soon reaches the riverside. Continue ahead close to the river until you come to a sign 'The Wildlife Trusts Northumberland Nature Reserve'. Walk ahead for about 30yds where you pass a series of metal bars on your left. After a further 20yds or so, you reach a clearing where you need to take the first path on your right and follow it a short way to a gate. Exit through the gate onto the minor road and turn left.

After a while, the road climbs quite steeply into Beltingham. Take special care at the sharp corner as you reach the top of the rise. The road arrives at a church and a cluster of attractive dwellings. Just a few strides beyond the church, take care to spot a fingerpost on the left, by a Victorian post box, which indicates 'Ridley ¼; Ridley Bridge ¾'.

Turn left at the post box and follow the path as it descends to cross a burn before rising between the trees and passing through a kissing gate. Continue along the top of the field keeping close to the fence on your right. You climb to a gate after which you arrive at a road. Turn left and follow the road as it descends to a junction at the entrance to Ridley Hall.

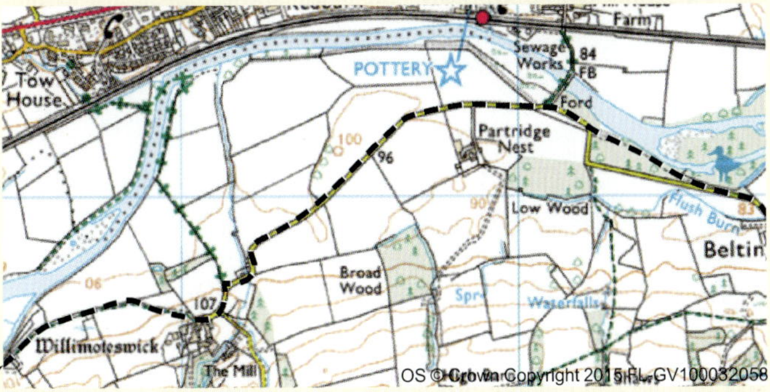

At the junction bear right to follow the sign 'Plankey Mill 3; Langley 3½' and walk ahead for ¼ mile to the National Trust (NT) Allen Banks and Staward car park and wc, located within the former walled garden of Ridley Hall.

(If time is pressing and/or following wet weather the surface conditions are poor, you may prefer to continue on the road for just over a mile, crossing a bridge over the River Allen and then climbing quite steeply until you reach an access road on the left to Tedcastle farm. A fingerpost (at times hidden by ferns) indicates, 'Lees Farm 1; Haydon

Beltingham

On your left you pass the charming old church dedicated to St Cuthbert, yet another site claimed to be a resting place of the saint's body on its 9th century journey from Lindisfarne to its eventual resting place in Durham. A more modern association is with the family of the late Queen Elizabeth the Queen Mother (1900-2002), the Bowes-Lyons, who were connected with the nearby Ridley Hall (see below) for over 100 years until 1948. An enclosed corner of the graveyard is reserved for the family. There are some ancient trees in the grounds, together with one planted by the late Queen Mother in 1989. There are some delightful properties in this quiet rural setting, including Beltingham House on the right with the Bowes-Lyon family initials engraved in the stone work.

St Cuthbert's at Beltingham

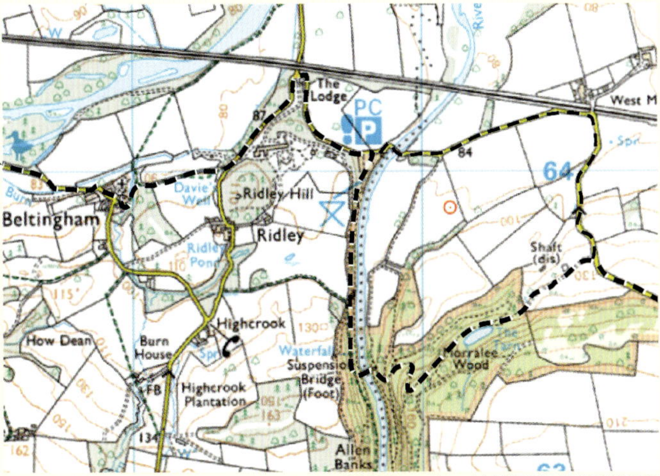

Bridge 2½'. Continue from (**A**) below. This route is about ½ mile shorter with less steep climbing.)

To continue on the trail, turn right into the car park (pay and display for non-National Trust members). You are now going to follow NT permissive paths through Allen Banks for about 1½ miles. Proceed straight ahead through the wooden shelter in which you will find some interesting information about the area. The clear path soon leads to the attractive riverside. As you walk ahead you pass a plaque marking the gift of

Path at Allen Banks
(*Photograph*: *Graeme Peacock*)

Ridley Hall

Originally belonging in the 16th century to the Ridley family of Willimoteswick Castle, the Hall has been burnt down, rebuilt and altered over the centuries. It has had several owners and a variety of uses. It passed into the Bowes-Lyon family in the late 19th century who owned it until the death of the Hon. Francis Bowes-Lyon in 1948. Currently it is a residential and conference centre and serves as a weekly boarding facility for some pupils of Haydon Bridge High School.

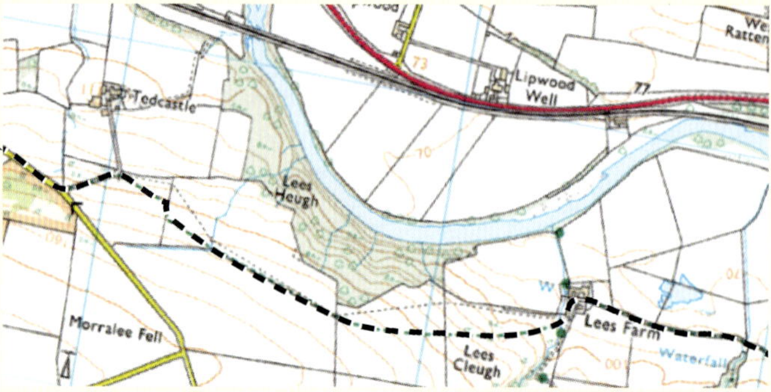

Allen Banks by the Hon. Francis Bowes-Lyon to the NT in 1942. After about ½ mile, you arrive at the aptly-named 'wobbly' bridge. This was severely damaged by floods but fortunately with the help of generous donations, the NT managed to restore and reopen the bridge in November 2014.

Cross the bridge and go straight ahead up two sets of steps. Turn right and follow the path as its ascends to a bench where you can take a well-earned rest. Continue ahead as the path zig-zags further upwards. At a T-junction, you meet a broad path. Turn left, walk about 10yds and then bear right to climb up the stepped path as indicated by the purple waymark.

Continue climbing until the path eventually descends towards a clearing. Turn sharp right at the sign 'Tarn'. Proceed up the broad path for about 200yds until you turn left at a further sign for the tarn. You go up more steps. Eventually as the path descends, a welcome bench provides the opportunity to have a rest and enjoy the splendid views. As you continue the descent, Morralee Tarn comes into view. Walk past the tarn. At the end of the tarn, on your right, a further bench gives you the opportunity to sit and admire the water lilies when in season.

To continue, return to the path, ignore a path off to the left (unless you want to return to the car park) and continue ahead on a broad green track. Just before a gate, you come to an information panel, *An inspiring landscape*, which tells of the artist, John Martin. You are, in fact, following part of the **John Martin Trail** which will lead you to his birthplace, Haydon Bridge, where you will be able to learn more of him.

Go through the kissing gate. The path is now indistinct in parts but make your way straight ahead for about 300yds to a further kissing gate that leads onto a road at a small

John Martin Trail

The waymarked heritage trail was created as a community project and officially opened in 2006. It covers places associated with Haydon Bridge's most famous son, the artist John Martin (1789-1854). Noted for his dramatic depictions of biblical stories, his paintings can be seen in Newcastle's Laing Art Gallery, as well as in the Tate Gallery in London. There is increasing interest in his work nationally and he is recognised locally in the form of this walk, information panels and a street named after him in Haydon Bridge.

parking area. (This is the road that leads from the NT car park entrance.)

Turn right and climb up the road for about 400yds until you reach an access road on the left to Tedcastle farm. A fingerpost (at times hidden by ferns) indicates, 'Lees Farm 1; Haydon Bridge 2½'.

(A) Proceed down the Tedcastle farm access road for about 200yds before turning right to cross a waymarked stile by a gate. After a few yards bear right up the faint track and climb to a ladder stile in a broken wall. Beware here before crossing to the other side of the wall, as the land there can be particularly boggy. You need to continue diagonally right to make your way to the wall/fence at the top of the field. Walk ahead with the wall on your right and make your way to the upper point of Lees Heugh Wood to reach a metal gate. Go through the gate and after a few paces you will see the buildings of Lees Farm below. Ahead to the left, the South Tyne reappears as it winds its way to Haydon Bridge, while to the right you may be able to see the battlements of 14th century Langley Castle (now an hotel and restaurant).

Don't descend too sharply towards the farm but aim to the right-hand side of the buildings. Proceed down the hillside to cross a waymarked ladderstile over a stone wall. Now descend diagonally right to the right-hand side of a clump of trees. Continue down in the same direction and follow the gorse bushes on your right passing a tree on your right. Bear right before the fence to find a gate in the corner where the fence meets a stone wall at a fingerpost 'Allen Banks 1'. Proceed through the gate and turn right past the farm buildings to exit onto an access road. Continue ahead

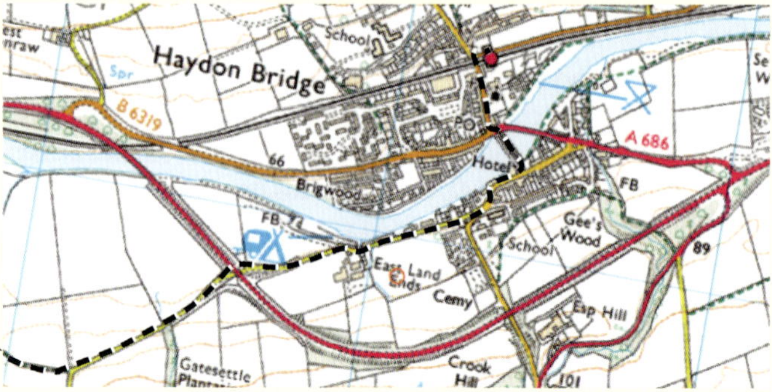

to meet a minor road. Bear left and follow the road which leads under the A69 **Haydon Bridge** bypass.

You pass a caravan site on the left and some converted farm buildings on the right. Here, at East Land Ends, the birthplace of the artist John Martin, an information panel provides details of his early life. Continue past a variety of dwellings until you reach a main road. Turn left, follow the road and then turn left just before the Anchor Hotel as Shaftoe Street becomes John Martin Street.

Cross the South Tyne over the now pedestrianised old bridge. An information panel on the bridge provides details of its chequered history. Just before the end of the bridge turn right to go down the subway steps. Before you walk through the subway, stop to enjoy the view of the river and both the old and new bridges. After you exit the subway, turn right into Church Street where you pass a fine war memorial and St Cuthbert's Church. (However, at this point

Haydon's Old Bridge *(Photograph: Graeme Peacock)*

Haydon Bridge

Haydon Bridge has long provided an important and busy river crossing point. Little is known of an early wooden bridge nor of the origins of the stone bridge which subsequently suffered a succession of damages and repairs from the great flood of 1771 onwards. By the mid-20th century, increasing traffic led in 1960 to a temporary steel replacement until the present concrete road bridge was opened in 1970. The attractive stone bridge now continues in use for pedestrians.

The long-awaited bypass which opened in 2009 restored much needed tranquillity to this pleasant little town which straddles both sides of the South Tyne. Here you can find a range of facilities including accommodation, a library with an internet café and, of course, the railway station.

The original village of Haydon lay slightly further north of the river and is marked today by the remains of a 12th century church which bears evidence of stonework from Hadrian's Wall. There are claims that the body of St Cuthbert may have rested here earlier on its long journey from Lindisfarne to its eventual burial place in Durham in 995. Appropriately the current parish church, consecrated in 1796, bears the saint's name.

should you wish to continue immediately onto Stage 9 to Warden, after you exit from the subway, turn sharp right and then almost immediately left). You then reach The Bridge (community library, visitor information point and internet café), and here you'll find a further information panel about Haydon Bridge's most famous son. The railway station lies a few yards ahead at the end of this stage of the Daft as a Brush Cancer Patient Care Walk.

Haydon Bridge War Memorial

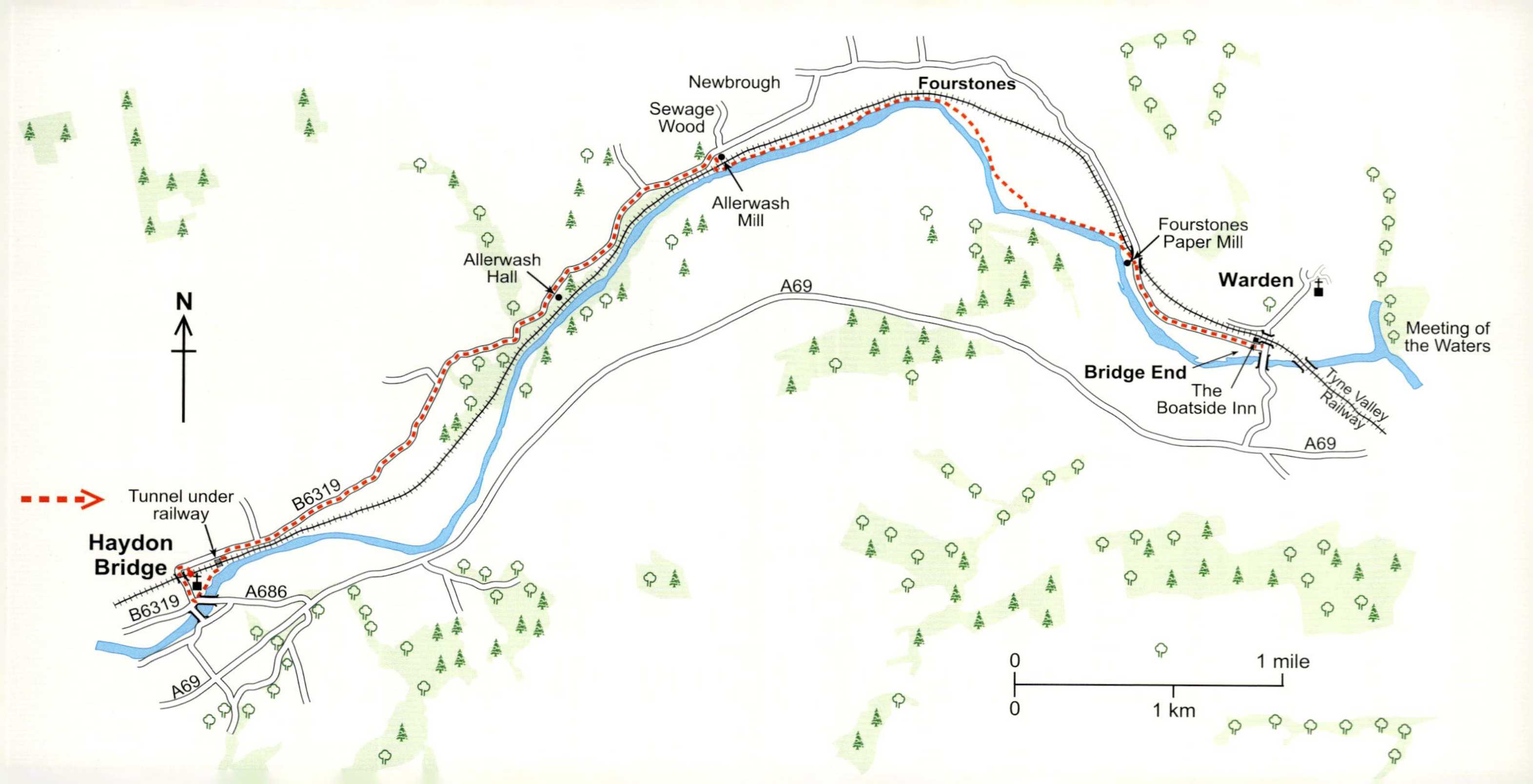

Newbrough
Fourstones
Sewage Wood
Allerwash Mill
Fourstones Paper Mill
Warden
Allerwash Hall
N
A69
Meeting of the Waters
Bridge End
The Boatside Inn
Tyne Valley Railway
A69
Tunnel under railway
B6319
Haydon Bridge
A686
B6319
A69
0
1 mile
0
1 km

STAGE 8
Haydon Bridge to Warden

6½ miles (10.5km)

Shortly after leaving Haydon Bridge, you join a minor road which you follow for about half the route. There are attractive views of the South Tyne Valley but the river itself is no longer visible for some time, although a line of trees below regularly marks its presence. The road leads past some interesting buildings before reaching a path which goes alongside the river for some 2 miles. You pass close to the small village of Fourstones where there are more fine properties. When the path rejoins the road for the final stretch of the walk, it may come as a surprise to encounter a large and long-established industrial plant, the Fourstones Paper Mill. The trail follows the roadside pavement to Warden, where the North and South Tyne routes converge very conveniently at The Boatside Inn, within a short distance of the meeting of the waters of the three Rivers Tyne. For the only time on the trail, there are no river crossings. With this stage being relatively short you may wish to combine it with a further stage. Conveniently, Hexham with train, bus and taxi links lies only 2¾ miles further ahead.

Entry/exit points	**Haydon Bridge (GR843645); Bridge End, Warden 6½ miles (10.5km)**
Map	**OS Explorer OL43 Hadrian's Wall**
Refreshments	**Pubs and The Bridge internet café in Haydon Bridge; The Boatside Inn at Warden**

The Walk

From the railway station, walk down Church Street past The Bridge (community library, visitor information point and internet café) and St Cuthbert's Church to the end of the street. Turn left and pause for a moment to view the road bridge which replaced the old stone bridge in 1970.

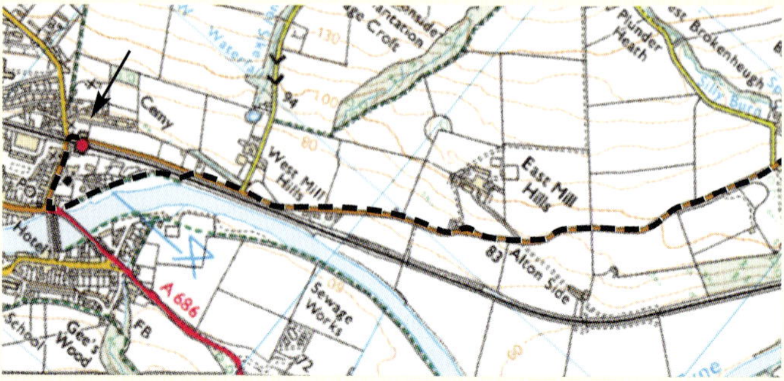

However, in turn, this has now been replaced to a large extent by the A69 bypass bridge which opened in 2009.

Don't proceed to the bridge but instead turn left after a few yards. A fingerpost on the right, sometimes partially hidden by foliage, directs you to Station Road (B6319) and also indicates that you are on the John Martin Heritage Trail again. You pass a picnic area as you walk along the surfaced path which takes you close to the railway line on the embankment above. After a couple of hundred yards, the path leads under the railway line onto a minor road (B6319).

Turn right and proceed ahead on the right-hand side of the road. You will be walking on this hedge-lined road for about 3 miles and you can make use of the narrow verge when appropriate. Initially the road climbs steadily before

Former A69 bridge

becoming more undulating. Trees become more in evidence, the road winds through a wooded area and after about 2 miles a sign indicates that you are at Allerwash. On your right you pass the high walls of Allerwash Hall which has its own short section of pavement. Shortly afterwards, near a gate, and unless it has sailed away, you might be surprised to find a yacht, the *Jenni B,* resting in a field!

You proceed past a collection of cottages and farm buildings as well as a road (Church Lane) on the left from Newbrough. The road descends and crosses the Newbrough Burn with some woods on your left with the unfortunate name of Sewage Wood! After a short distance, turn right at the fingerpost 'Fourstones 1; Warden Bridge End 3'. Follow the path as it goes to the right of the property (Allerwash Mill), ignore the metal gate on the left and go down the steps towards the Newbrough Burn. Turn left to go under the bridge and there at last is the South Tyne!

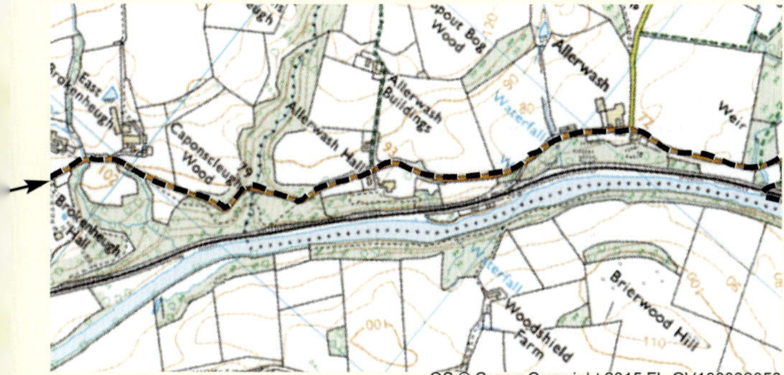

Turn left to clamber up to a narrow path running alongside the river. Proceed along the path for a couple of hundred yards or so. Just after a clump of trees go through the gap in the wall on your left, turn right and walk in the same direction. (This slight diversion avoids an eroded part of the path.) Soon after passing under telephone wires, bear right to rejoin the riverside path. Proceed ahead. Soon you pass an engraved stone bench on your left. Continue as the path bears slightly left between the trees. Walk past a cottage and some old farm buildings and carry on to the right of a waymarked gate.

When you reach a large house, walk over the grass to the right of the building. This is one of the many fine properties at Fourstones where solar panels seem popular. Continue ahead with a fence on your left until you go over a ladder

Near Fourstones

stile. The path goes through a kissing gate a little further away from the river. Shortly, the broad path bears towards a gate; however, some 5 yards before the gate, you need to turn right onto a much narrower path which soon leads to a stile. It's not long before you are walking once more alongside the river. Care is needed as the path is narrow and the bank is steep in parts. Watch your footing as some creatures have been making holes along the route! Eventually you emerge onto a road at a point just to the right of the level crossing warning lights.

Turn right and walk along the pavement to pass the Fourstones Paper Mill complex. The company has been making specialist paper since 1763. Carry on along the road which, initially, has no pavement. Take care here as you are

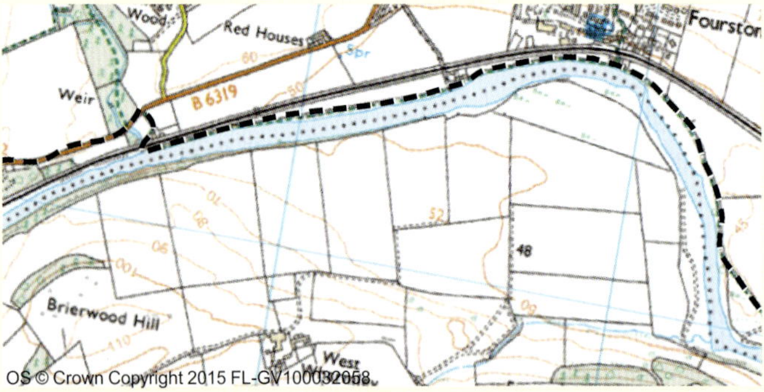

Waters meet – now together!

metalled path to a gate at a railway crossing. Just before the gate, turn left, then bear right. Follow the path nearest to the riverside through Tyne Green with Tynedale Golf Course on the right.

Hexham Bridge (1793) comes into sight and you may see some rowing crews on the river. You pass a children's play area as you remain close to the riverside. Eventually, with the boathouses on your right, turn right just before the bridge and then bear left to make your way to the main road.

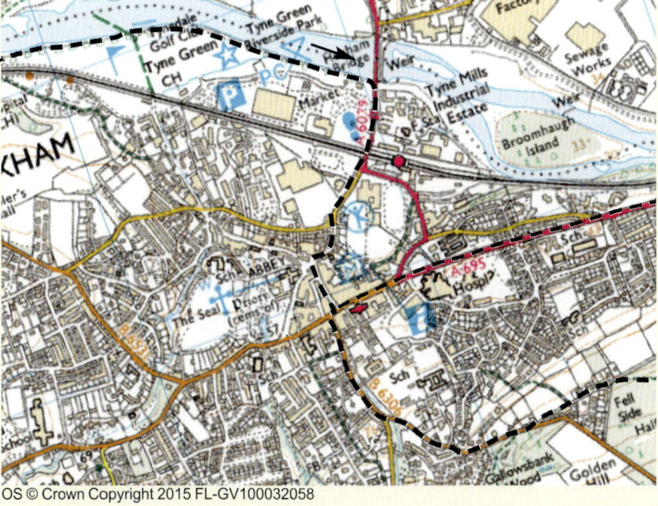

Approaching Hexham (*Photograph: Graeme Peacock*)

Turn right and follow the pavement, going over the railway bridge and passing a mini-roundabout (the station lies to the left) to arrive at some pedestrian lights. Cross over to the other side of the road and turn right. Now follow the pavement as it climbs steeply into **Hexham**. At the top of Hallstile Bank, turn left into the Market Place and there on the right is Hexham Abbey. On your left is the historic Gatehouse or Moot Hall.

To continue, walk up pedestrianised Fore Street and just before the HSBC bank, bear right to meet the main road (A695).

Hexham

Hexham, in the county of Northumberland, is the first major market town encountered on the walk. Its location, just beyond the confluence of the North and South Tyne rivers in the picturesque Tyne Valley, together with its Saxon abbey and other attractions, makes it a popular destination for visitors from within and outside the region.

Historically, the development of the town has been closely interwoven with that of the abbey. The abbey itself has had a long and chequered history since its original foundation in around 674 by St Wilfrid as a monastery under Benedictine rule. It was laid waste by the Vikings in the 9th century, refounded as an Augustinian priory in the early 12th century, gutted by the Scots in 1296 and, finally, lost its monastic

significance in Henry V111's Dissolution of 1537. Happily, it continued as a parish church, worship taking place in the surviving chapel and transept areas. A nave was added in the early 20th century. Now we see a substantial and elegant parish church containing a fascinating blend of ancient and modern features including the Refectory café.

Today the abbey stands, rather like a spiritual oasis, in the centre of the town, surrounded by pleasant grounds, bustling streets and a market place. Hexham has a variety of shopping and leisure facilities and has good rail and public transport links. The Tourist Information Office, public toilets, car park and railway station, can be found through the Gatehouse.

Hexham Racecourse, Northumberland's only racecourse and England's most northerly National Hunt venue, lies two miles south of the town centre.

Hexham Abbey and market (*Photograph: Graeme Peacock*)

(If you are pressed for time and/or it has been very wet you may prefer to walk along the roadside path to Dilston. In this case turn left and follow the A695 Corbridge road for 2½ miles to Dilston Bridge, see (**A**) below, saving ½ mile.)

Otherwise, to continue on the main trail, turn right at the main road and then use the pedestrian lights to cross to the other side. Turn left and after a few yards turn right to walk up Eastgate. When convenient cross the road and continue on the left-hand side pavement. After about ¼ mile, bear left at the fork in the road to continue climbing for a about a further ¼ mile to arrive at Fellside. Turn left along the access road, passing a pleasant row of cottages with views over the town. On the right, some 10yds beyond a vehicle turning space at the remains of an old quarry, take the public footpath 'Dukes House ¾'.

Follow the narrow path as it rises, levels out, descends and then resumes climbing past a couple of waymarks. The now broader path becomes stony as it rises quite steeply before levelling off to pass a clearing and reach an access road. Turn left in the direction 'Dilston 1½' and follow the broad tree-lined track which passes Duke's House with its ornate chimney pots. The current property is a refurbished Victorian house said to have been built on the site of a house belonging to the Duke of Portland, and hence so named.

The access road becomes a narrow and at times an uneven path which in wet weather may become particularly muddy. Ignore paths off. At the end of the wood, follow the path as it bears left with a field on the right and a further field on the left beyond the bushes. The narrow path descends to an access track. Cross over and continue ahead on what is now a broader path to reach a road. Cross over the road and go through a gate. You pass Dilston Scout Camp on your right and then Dilston Physic Garden on the left. Notices provide details of this "tranquil place to unwind".

You meet a further access road at a former mill, now a B&B, beyond which runs the river, known as 'Devil's Water', which will soon accompany you as it flows to join the Tyne. On the other side of the river, but not visible, are the remains of Dilston Castle, the ancestral seat of the Earl of Derwentwater who was executed in 1716 for his part the previous year in the Jacobite Rebellion.

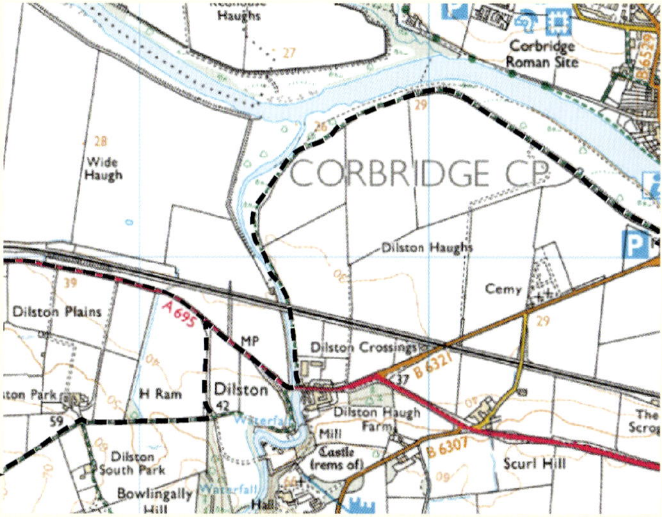

OS © Crown Copyright 2015 FL-GV100032058

Turn left to walk a short distance to the main road (A695) which you need to cross with great care **(A)**. Turn right and walk across Dilston Bridge over Devil's Water.

At the end of the bridge turn immediately left at the public footpath sign "Corbridge 1¾". Follow the path with Devil's Water on your left to some steps that climb to a gate at the side of the railway. Take extreme care to cross over the railway lines. Continue ahead, until some 100yds after

Devil's Water enters the Tyne

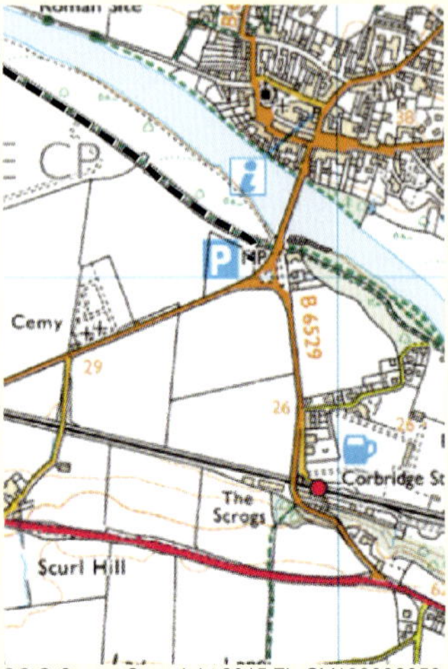

OS © Crown Copyright 2015 FL-GV100032058

passing beneath some overhead power lines, you see a gate on the left. Go down a faint path and pass through the gate. Turn right and follow the path until you come to the confluence of Devil's Water with the Tyne.

The path bears right, passes some gorse bushes and goes through a gateway. Follow the path for about 550yds before bearing left onto a narrower path that goes to the left of the trees and close to the riverside. (The path is becoming eroded in parts and if the river is high it is advisable to follow one of the more inland paths.) After about a further 250yds, look out for a clearing in the trees through which you should see a stone structure which is worth the short detour. The stones were originally part of a huge ramp which carried a Roman road up a carriageway onto a bridge over the river. An information panel provides details. The remains of the Roman town of Corstopitum are on the other side of the river.

Corbridge ahead

Proceed ahead along the riverside path. On the opposite side of the river you should be able to make out the tower of the noted parish church of St Andrew (see below). Just before the bridge at **Corbridge**, turn right to leave the riverside and go through a gate on the embankment (there is a convenient car park to the right) to meet a road at the south end of the bridge. The village centre with its pleasant amenities lies over the bridge, while the starting point of Stage 10 of the trail is just to the left of Lion Court apartments on the opposite side of the road. (There is a one way system for traffic on the bridge so use the traffic lights to cross the road.) However, this stage of the Daft as a Brush Cancer Patient Care Walk now ends here.

Corbridge

A visit to the centre of Corbridge, situated at the north end of Corbridge Bridge, enables you to enjoy the attractions of this fascinating village. The bridge itself dates from 1674 and was the only Tyne bridge not destroyed by the terrible flood of 1771.

Corbridge has a market place and this is dominated by the parish church of St Andrew, "which is the most important surviving Saxon monument in Northumberland, except for Hexham crypt" (Pevsner, 1992). It is possible that the Saxon builders made use of stones from the nearby Roman great camp of Corstopitum. Corstopitum also provided a convenient source of material for other buildings, including the 14th century Vicar's Pele, built in the churchyard as a defence against Scots' incursions. The site can be visited a short distance west of Corbridge.

Today, these and other historic features, as well as its various eating places and traditional and boutique shops, have contributed to the popularity of the village as a place to visit. It is also seen as an attractive place to live. Its location, 18 miles from Newcastle, and road and rail improvements, means that many residents now commute to work in the Newcastle and Gateshead conurbation. It has also become a fashionable place for retired people to live. The railway station lies about ½ mile south of the bridge.

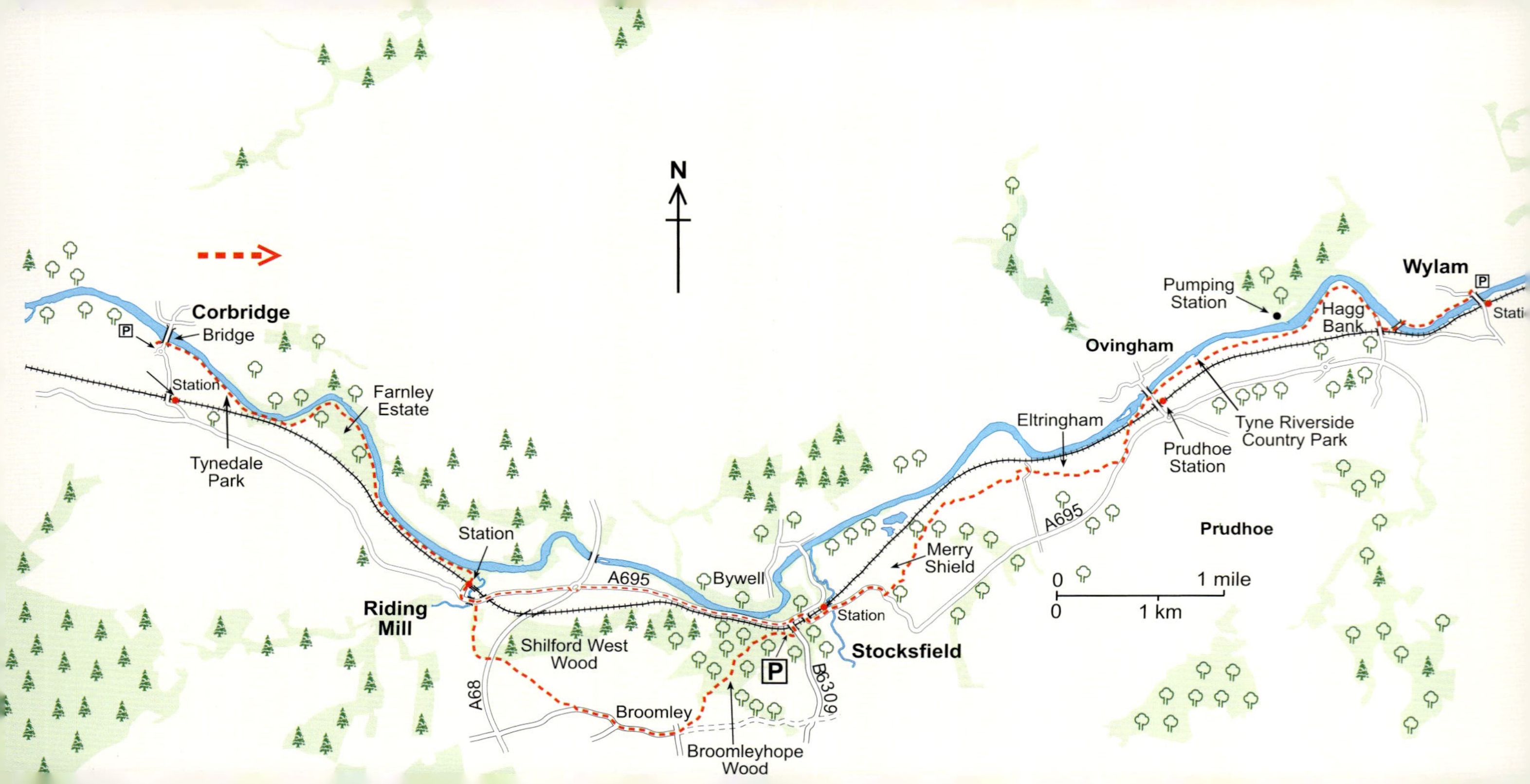
N
Corbridge
Bridge
Station
Tynedale Park
Farnley Estate
Station
Riding Mill
A68
Shilford West Wood
A695
Bywell
Broomley
Broomleyhope Wood
B6309
P
Station
Stockfield
Merry Shield
A695
Eltringham
Prudhoe
Prudhoe Station
Tyne Riverside Country Park
Ovingham
Pumping Station
Hagg Bank
Wylam
0
1 mile
0
1 km

STAGE 10
Corbridge to Wylam

13¼ miles (21.3km)

A section of Stage 10 has had to be diverted. See www.daftasabrush.org.uk for amended route.

This stage of the trail closely follows the Tyne most of the way on pleasant undulating green paths. At times, with several climbs including some sustained ascents, this can seem a fairly long walk. However, several convenient exit points near to railway stations and bus stops could help to accommodate the trail to your needs. These entry/exits are at the relatively small and attractive urban areas along the Tyne Valley which are much favoured by commuters to the more industrialised areas of Tyneside that you will encounter later. At Riding Mill, the trail climbs through delightful woodland and crosses some farmland before descending towards Stocksfield. However, if time is pressing and the weather conditions are unfavourable there is the alternative of a more direct route along a roadside path. There are six river crossings in this stage of the trail, one of which you cross.

Entry/exit points	Corbridge (GR989641); Riding Mill 3 miles (4.8km); Stocksfield 6 miles (9.7km); Prudhoe 9 miles (14.5km); Wylam 13¼ miles (21.3km)
Maps	OS Explorer OL43 Hadrian's Wall; OS Explorer 316 Newcastle upon Tyne
Refreshments	Cafés and pubs in Corbridge; hotel in Riding Mill; riverside café at Prudhoe; pubs and tearoom in Wylam

The walk

This stage of the trail begins from Corbridge at the south-east end of the bridge at the access road in front of the Lion Court apartments. Go over the stone stile to the left of the apartments at the fingerpost indicating 'Farnley Grange 1; Broomhaugh via Farnley Scar 3'. Follow the track that leads through a waymarked kissing gate. The tree-lined path is criss-crossed by a number of paths. Keep on the path

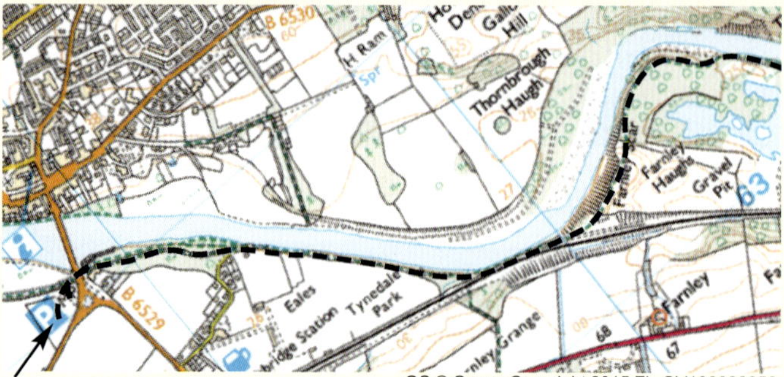

nearest to river until you arrive at a fence where you need to turn right and then left to go through a gateway. Continue ahead to the end of the wall.

There are two paths ahead. Sports fans may prefer the higher path along the embankment which gives good views over Tynedale Park, home to Corbridge Cricket Club and Tynedale Rugby Club. This is also an important venue for car boot sales and festivals ranging from camping to classic cars. However, to keep closer to the river, follow the lower path which eventually bears right, via a short stony section, onto the broad embankment at the end of the sports field. Continue ahead. The path gets close to the Newcastle-Carlisle railway line before

Checking the route

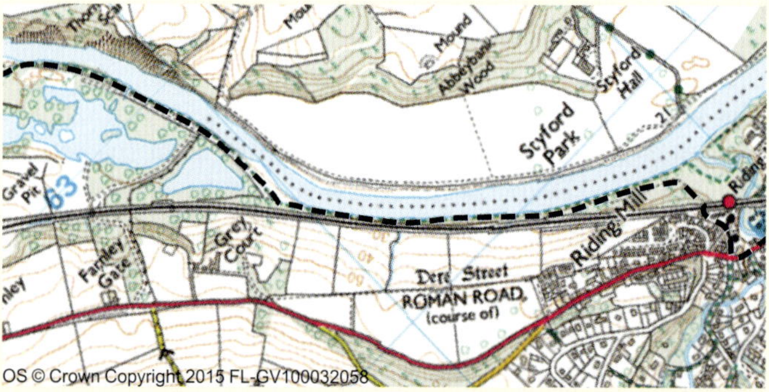

returning to the riverside. As you walk along the riverside, the path narrows and you need to be sure-footed, particularly along a couple of short stony sections. When the river begins to swing to the left, go up a set of steps on your right and turn left to climb a further set of steep steps adjacent to an old railway tunnel.

After a further steep climb and steps, the path levels off before descending quite steeply between wire fences. In the river, you may spot a solitary pillar, a relic of a former bridge. Ignore paths to your right through the trees. As you proceed ahead you may notice reference to fishing rights on the Farnley Estate through which you are now passing. A lake appears on the right. After several hundred yards, you go through a waymarked gap in a wall. The path narrows and after a while it bears left and re-enters a wooded area.

Cross a stile as the path proceeds between the railway line and the river. Again care needs to be taken as the path drops quite sharply at times. Continue ahead across two small footbridges.

Eventually, you come to a junction of paths and a waymarked post. Unfortunately, as there is no right of way between Riding Mill and Stocksfield, the trail now needs to go inland. Turn right and walk up the slope of the permissive path to reach a kissing gate into Riding Mill Station. Turn left along the platform, cross the bridge, exit the station, walk ahead and bear left along Dene Terrace. At the main road (A695) turn left to pass (or visit) The Wellington (hotel, restaurant and bar).

Continue ahead on the left-hand side pavement. You soon reach a junction on your right and you need to cross over the main road with care to Whiteside Bank.

(However, if time is pressing and/or following wet weather the surface conditions are poor, you may prefer to continue along the path by the side of the A695 for the next 2 miles – saving a mile! After leaving

Riding Mill

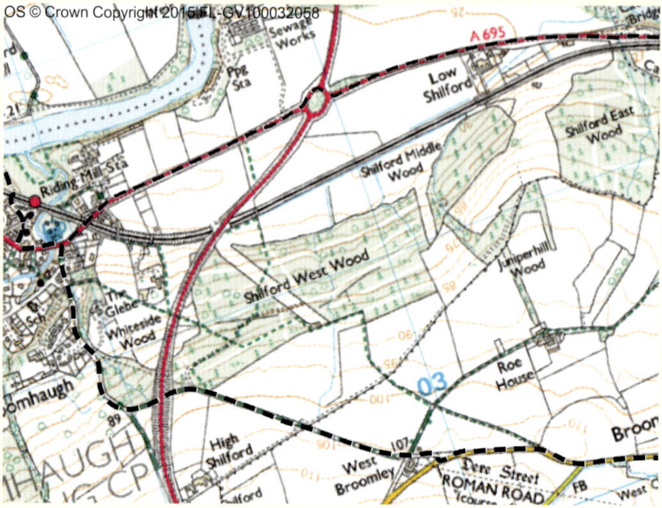

Riding Mill, cross over the road when convenient and continue ahead on the right-hand side pavement. You pass a roundabout and junction with the A68. At a layby you need to cross to the other side of the road and pick up the roadside path again. Shortly afterwards, the main route emerges on the right from the B6309 Ebchester road to join the roadside path – see (**A**) below).

To continue on the trail, walk up Whiteside Bank for about 100 yards and turn left, immediately past Whiteside Cottage, at the fingerpost, 'Broomley 1¼'. The narrow path climbs steeply. You cross a waymarked stile. Walk diagonally right across the field, on the faint path, towards the right-hand side of the property just visible between the trees (Wentworth Grange Nursing and Residential Care Home). Continue around the side of the property and walk ahead to a gate in the fence. Go through the gate and climb up the steps to reach the

Broomleyhope Wood

main road (A68). Take extremely great care to cross this busy, fast road.

A fingerpost suggests that Broomley is now 1½ miles away (and it may be even a little further!). Proceed ahead, go through the kissing gate and walk between the paddock fences. Go over the waymarked stile and enter the woods. You will find that the route is generally well waymarked from now onwards. Walk ahead, cross a vehicular track and continue to climb steadily. At a T-junction of paths, turn left and follow the now more level path. At another T-junction, turn right to resume climbing again with a fence on your left. The path leads past a stone-cladded pumping station on your left and you arrive at a stile at the edge of the woods.

Cross the stile, turn left and proceed ahead along the edge of the field. A small plank crossing leads into a second field. Continue ahead to walk around the edge of two sides of the field until you meet a broad track with a gate in the wall directly ahead. Go through the gate and continue ahead along the narrow field-edge path with a wire fence on your

left. Exit the field at the top left-hand corner through a narrow opening to meet a minor road with a fingerpost on your right. Cross over the minor road and go over the stile. Continue ahead with the fence on your left. At the end of the field, go over the ladder stile to arrive at a road. Cross to the other side of the road and turn left. You now need to walk, with due care, along the road for about 500 yards. However, there is a grass verge should you encounter traffic. The road takes you through the neat hamlet of Broomley.

As the road turns right at a junction, take care to cross straight over to join a broad public byway. Walk about 40 yards and turn left to go over a stile by the fingerpost 'Stocksfield 1¼'. Bear diagonally right as indicated by the fingerpost and walk towards the power-line post with a pond over to your right. As you proceed, the faint green path is about 20yds from the fence on the left. You pass a small waymarked post near the edge of the woods. Enter the woods, descending to cross a small footbridge over the Smithy Burn. Climb to cross a stile and follow the path with a fence on your right and the burn below on the left. Turn right at a waymark as the path leaves the burn. Ignoring a faint path to the right, bear left at a fork and keep on the clearer path between the trees. After about 75 yards, at a T-junction, turn left and continue on the broad path through the ancient woodland. In parts, this can be muddy after heavy rain.

You meet a fingerpost 'Stocksfield 1' where you follow the path as it bears left. Walk across the duck-boarding, which helps to avoid a particularly muddy section, and continue straight ahead. Ignore paths off as the path narrows and you descend through a clearing. The path leads to a small car park which you enter through a gap in the hedge on the right. Proceed through the car park and turn left on the minor road (B6309 Ebchester) and go over the railway bridge to meet a busy road (A695). Cross the road with care to join the pavement and turn right. The alternative route from Riding Mill along the roadside converges with the main route at this point (**A**).

Although this is a busier section of road, during its final stretch you should at least get a glimpse of the river. At a junction, ignore the road on the left to Bywell, and continue alongside the main road to walk through Stocksfield. Soon after the railway station, you are in more open country.

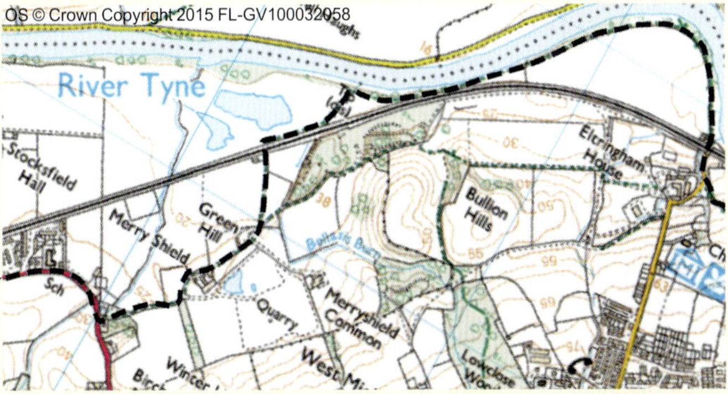

Shortly after passing Stocksfield Cricket Club, turn left onto a lane. Ignore paths off and carry on past the farm buildings (Merry Shield). There are traces of a former quarry on the right. Go through a waymarked gate and through the tunnel under the railway line. Turn right and walk ahead. There is a large pond to the left. Follow the line of the woodland on the right; you will probably hear trains thundering along the railway beyond. You arrive at a metal gate on your right. Go through the gate, down the steps and across the footbridge to a waymark. Carry on with the river once again nearby as you pass another salmon fishing area (Eltringham Fishings).

Eventually, you will see a number of 'canny' cabins on the other side of the river. These are located just before the

Salmon fishing area

Ovingham Bridges

village of Ovingham. You arrive at a railway crossing. Observe the instructions to cross the railway with very careful attention to the warning lights. Proceed uphill. At a crossing of paths turn left at the sign 'Restricted Byway Eltringham ½'. The path climbs steeply and you pass a fairly modern property. Continue ahead ignoring a sign to Prudhoe on the right. The path exits onto an access road. Turn right and then left at the Hammerite factory to follow the narrow path alongside the factory railings with the bushes and the road to your right.

At the end of the industrial plant turn left at the public footpath sign 'Tyne Riverside Park ¼'. Proceed ahead, with the metal railings on your left, and follow the path as it descends towards the river, passing a couple of Woodland Trust signs. You reach the railway line. Cross the line with the usual care and continue to descend towards the river. Follow the path, with the river on your left to reach an entrance to the Tyne Countryside Park car park. The trail carries straight on.

However, depending on season/time, refreshments maybe available at the park café (Café@Prudhoe Riverside) which is reached via the car park. Prudhoe Station is to the right of the car park entrance.

Across the river is Ovingham where St Mary the Virgin's Church boasts a late-Saxon west tower and is the burial place of the noted artist and engraver Thomas Bewick. The

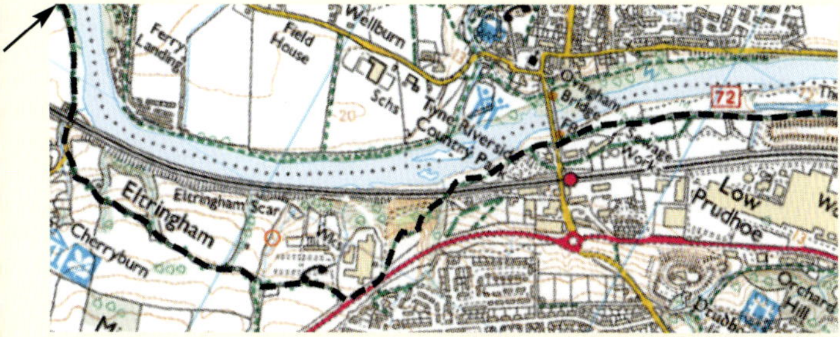

OS © Crown Copyright 2015 FL-GV100032058

bridge which you can see dates from 1883 when it replaced a ford and a ferry service. The nature of its construction results in a lot of noise as vehicles go across. The adjacent footbridge is a more modern crossing (1974).

To continue on the trail, walk ahead on the surfaced track signed 'Hagg Bank 1¾; Wylam 2¼' and go under the bridges. After about 200yds, leave the track and bear left towards the riverside where you will pick up a narrow but well-trodden path. Now make your way ahead close to the river for several hundred yards. After a small footbridge you come close to the surfaced track again but unless the conditions are muddy, bear left and continue closer to the river. Eventually, the path bears right and you rejoin the surfaced track.

Continue ahead along the track. On the other side of the river, you will see a prominent tower, part of the 19th century Wylam Pumping Station. The trail climbs quite

19th century pumping station

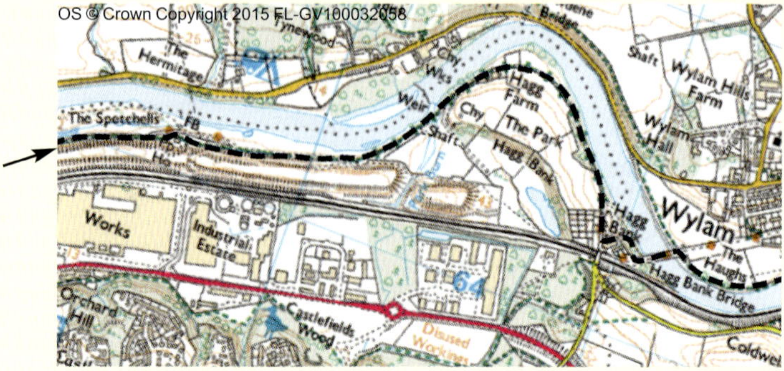

steeply. As the track descends, you pass some fine property. You go through a paddock area where the cattle grids serve as barriers to the horses which you may see there. Carry on until you arrive at what is the back of a Tyne Riverside Country Park sign. Ahead, at the foot of Hagg Bank is a sign for Cycleway 72. However, don't proceed up the bank but instead leave the main track and fork left. Walk along the clear path which returns towards the riverside. Follow the path, which can be narrow and steeply cambered in parts, until it climbs to arrive at Hagg Bank Bridge.

Wylam

The small, pretty village of Wylam is now a pleasant place to live, with easy commuting to NewcastleGateshead. This contrasts with its industrial past when it was heavily involved in the extraction of coal and iron, being described by one late Victorian commentator as the very worst colliery village he had seen. Wylam Station is one of the oldest stations still in use. The former station master's house (1835) is a listed building; a plaque commemorates William Hedley, who attended school here and is famous as the inventor of the locomotive Puffing Billy. George Stephenson, sometimes called the "father of the railways" and Timothy Hackforth, an engineer, were born here and carried out pioneering work in the development of steam locomotion.

On the walk we crossed the Wylam Railway Bridge of 1876 (Hagg Bank Bridge), now disused but pedestrianised, which provided a link with the Newcastle to Carlisle railway; its single-span arch is reminiscent of Newcastle's Tyne Bridge. Later, on the next stage, we pass the humble cottage where George Stephenson was born. It is owned by the National Trust and is open to the public.

Turn left and cross this delightful bridge which, from 1876 to 1968, carried the railway from North Wylam Station to join the Newcastle-Carlisle railway. An information panel at the far end provides details. Once over the bridge, turn immediately right down the steps back to the riverside. Proceed ahead, ignoring paths off, until the path turns sharp left to pass some allotments (this way avoids an eroded section to the right). Follow the path as it climbs to

Hagg Bridge (*Photograph: Graeme Peacock*)

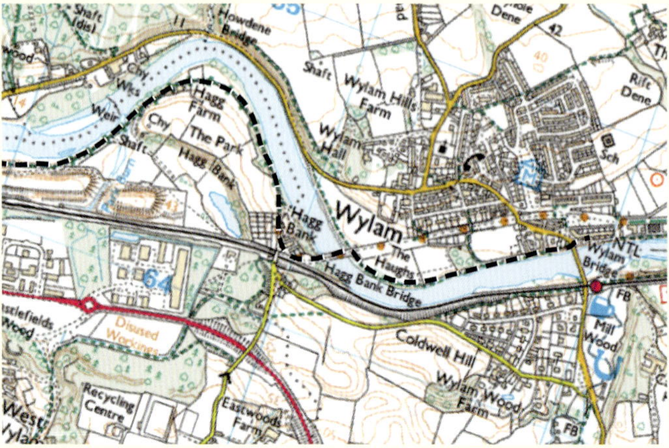

a junction and bear right to arrive at the cricket field. Turn right and take the path back into the woods.

Turn left to walk along by a fence and the sports field on your left. Continue straight ahead past a terrace of houses and go down some steps for the final section along the riverside. The path leads under Wylam Bridge (1836) and

Wylam Bridge

you climb to an access road where you turn left. (The main road leads on the left across the bridge to Wylam Station and the Boathouse "arguably the Best Pub in the World"!, while to the right it leads to the village and its amenities). Follow the access road passing the war memorial on your left. Turn right into the Riverside Country Park car park and walk ahead to an information panel 'Wylam Car Park' behind which is a fingerpost. This is the end of this stage of the Daft as Brush Cancer Patient Care Walk.

Wylam War Memorial

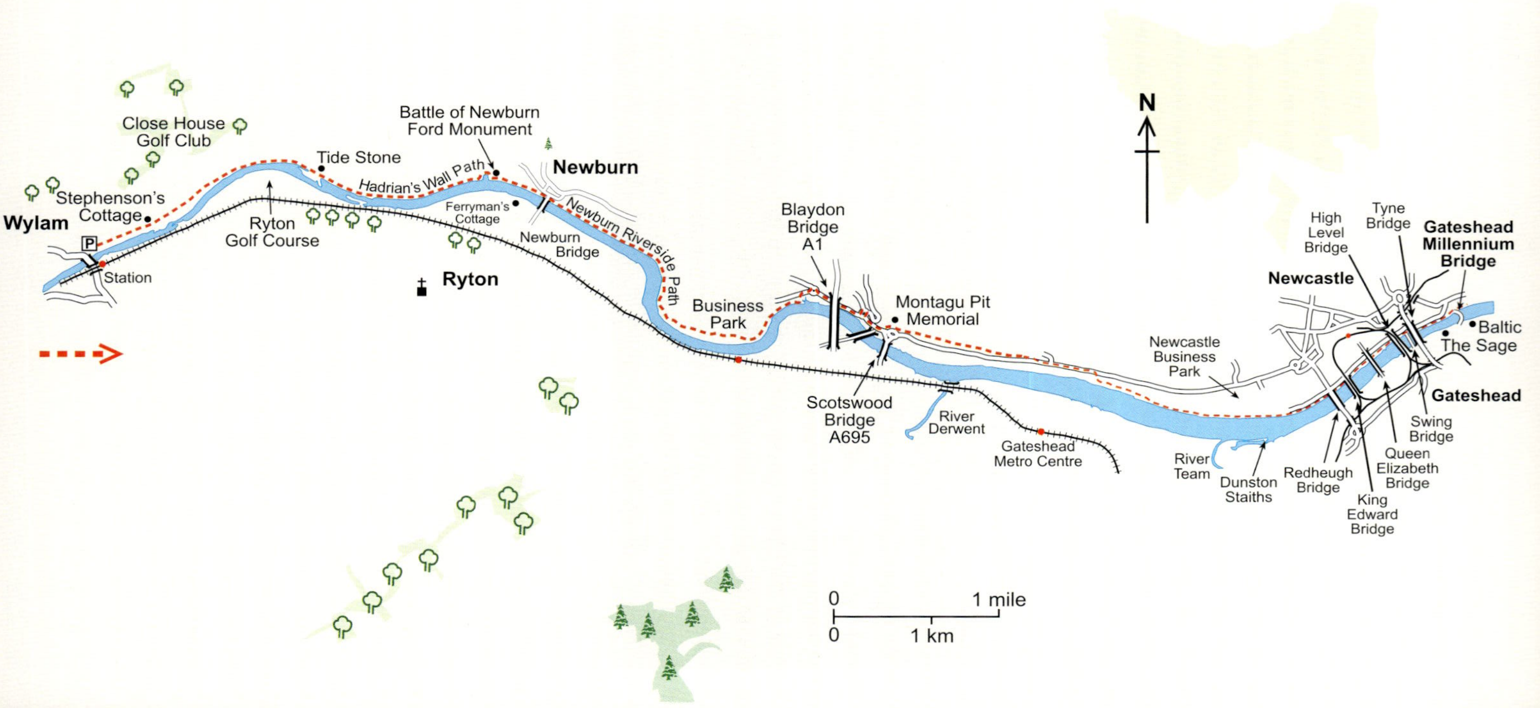

Close House Golf Club
Battle of Newburn Ford Monument
Tide Stone
Hadrian's Wall Path
Newburn
Stephenson's Cottage
Wylam
P
Station
Ryton Golf Course
Ferryman's Cottage
Newburn Bridge
Newburn Riverside Path
Ryton
Blaydon Bridge A1
Business Park
Montagu Pit Memorial
Scotswood Bridge A695
River Derwent
Gateshead Metro Centre
N
Newcastle Business Park
High Level Bridge
Tyne Bridge
Gateshead Millennium Bridge
Newcastle
Baltic
The Sage
Gateshead
Swing Bridge
Queen Elizabeth Bridge
King Edward Bridge
Redheugh Bridge
Dunston Staiths
River Team
0
1 mile
0
1 km

STAGE 11
Wylam to NewcastleGateshead

10¾ miles (17.3km)

The trail now begins to approach urban Tyneside. It commences with a delightful stroll along the riverside from Wylam to Newburn which could be undertaken on either side of the Tyne. However, for the purposes of this trail, you proceed down the north side to pass the birthplace of the famous railway engineer, George Stephenson. From Newburn onwards the trail is on surfaced paths almost entirely close to the river which, since leaving Wylam, has become tidal. There is clear evidence of regeneration where former power stations and industrial sites have been replaced by office buildings and modern housing. You will be reminded of the importance of William (Lord) Armstrong to the industrial heritage of Tyneside. There are eleven river crossings on this stage of the trail, all of which are encountered, as the trail approaches the twin settlements of Newcastle and Gateshead and you arrive at the iconic Gateshead Millennium Bridge.

Entry/exit points	Wylam (GR112643); Newburn 3¼ miles (5.2km); NewcastleGateshead Quaysides 10¾ miles (17.3km)
Map	OS Explorer 316 Newcastle upon Tyne
Refreshments	Pubs and tearoom in Wylam; riverside café and pubs at Newburn; cafés in Newburn Industrial Estate and Newburn Riverside, pubs and cafés on Newcastle and Gateshead Quaysides

The walk

The walk starts at the information panel 'Wylam Car Park' on the site of the former North Wylam Station (1876-1968). Here you can read about Wylam's history in the early development of the railways. A fingerpost 'Hadrian Cycleway 72' shows that your first destination, Newburn, is

2 miles away; however, a small sign nearby is perhaps much nearer the truth when it indicates 3 miles!

Proceed ahead in the direction of Newburn, through a fence and across an access road along the mid-18th century waggonway. After about ½ mile you reach the birthplace of the noted railway engineer George Stephenson (1781-1848). The cottage is a National Trust property and together with

George Stephenson (1781-1848)

George Stephenson was born at Wylam. With no money for schooling, he followed his father into working with stationary engines in local collieries and attended classes to learn to read and write. His fascination with machines led him to teach himself in his spare time how these engines worked (by taking them apart and reassembling them!). Promotion soon followed and in 1812 he was made responsible for the maintenance of all of the machinery at Killingworth Colliery.

There, in 1814, he built his first railway locomotive *Blucher* named after the Prussian General Blucher. Stephenson's reputation grew and in 1823 he set up in partnership, with his only son Robert and others, as Robert Stephenson and Company, the first locomotive works in the world. *Locomotion* was their first locomotion engine. Another success came when the *Stephensons' Rocket* won a trial held by the directors of the proposed Liverpool & Manchester Railway. George Stephenson also designed some of the bridges needed for the early railway lines. In 1847 he became the first president of the Institution of Mechanical Engineers. A magnificent monument to him (Lough, 1862) is located, appropriately, near Newcastle Central Station.

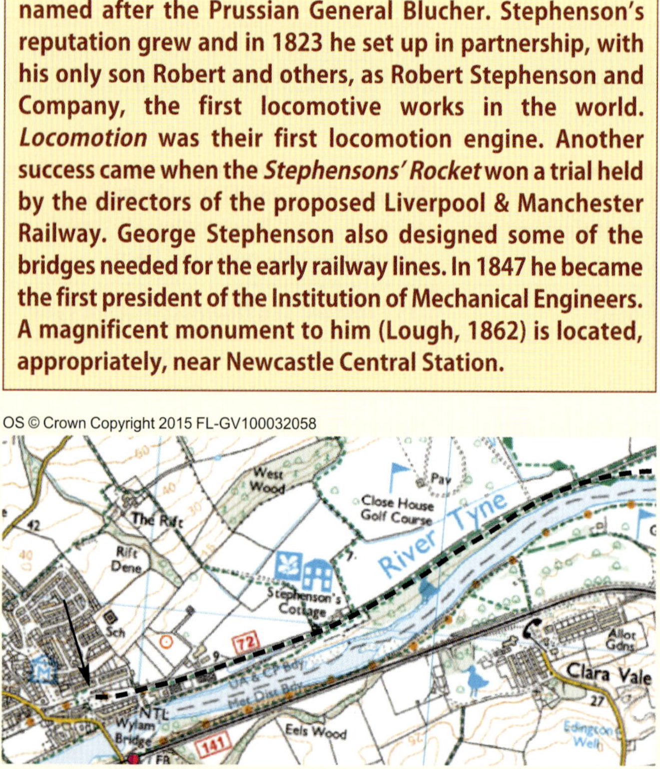

Stephenson's Cottage *(Photograph: Graeme Peacock)*

its café is open to visitors at regular times as indicated on the noticeboard.

Opposite the cottage, turn right through the kissing gate and walk a short distance to go through a further kissing gate in the fence on your left. You have now joined the pleasant riverside path that leads ahead to Newburn. However, care needs to be exercised in some areas due to the erosion of the bankside.

After a further 200yds or so, you come to an open space where the path forks. Take the left-hand fork and follow the grassy path which leads between trees. From here onwards, ignore paths off to the left unless you wish to return to the nearby waggonway in case of inclement weather or the need to make haste. At a junction of paths keep straight ahead close to the fence on your left. Close House Golf Course and

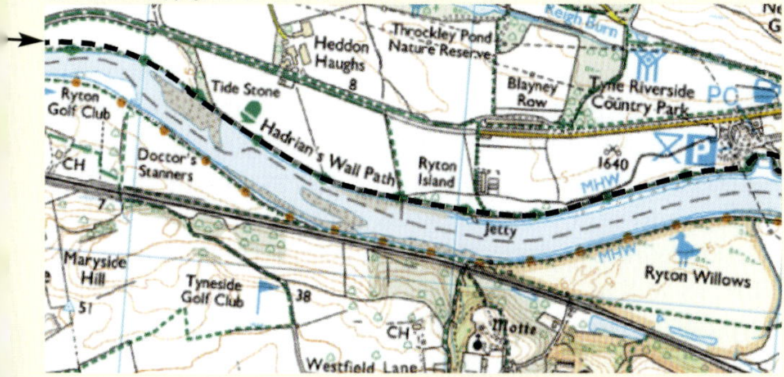

Pleasant riverside path to Newburn

the football and rugby pitches used by Newcastle University lie beyond the waggonway.

Eventually the narrow path veers right to reach a field and goes along the right-hand field edge. Here care needs to be taken as parts of the bankside have been particularly subject to erosion. Further downstream, across the river to your right, you should be able to see the spire of Ryton Parish Church. At the end of the field bear left onto the higher of two paths. As the path descends to meet the lower path, look out for a wooden fence on your left in front of which there is an old stone marker, the Tide Stone. You can just make out the date, 1785, and the three-castles emblem of Newcastle Corporation. The stone indicated the town boundary at that time, as well as the point at which the Tyne was tidal until dredging moved the limit further upstream nearer to Wylam around 1900.

Tide Stone

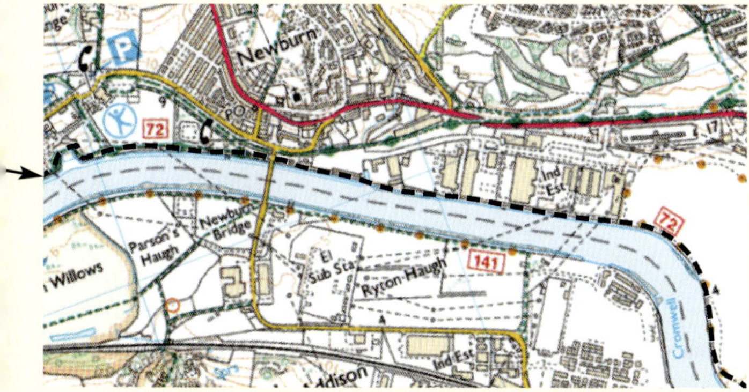

Continue ahead on the tree-lined riverside path with a wire fence and a field on your left. Eventually, towards the end of the field, bear left and follow the broader path as it climbs to pass a black pole and arrive at a kissing gate. Go through the gate, turn right and continue along a surfaced path. On the opposite bank, a white house (Ferryman's Cottage) marks the site of a former ferry crossing. You arrive at a junction where a signpost indicates one more mile to Newburn, while the acorn symbol tells you that you are joining a National Trail (Hadrian's Wall Path). A panel

Ferryman's Cottage *(Photograph: Graeme Peacock)*

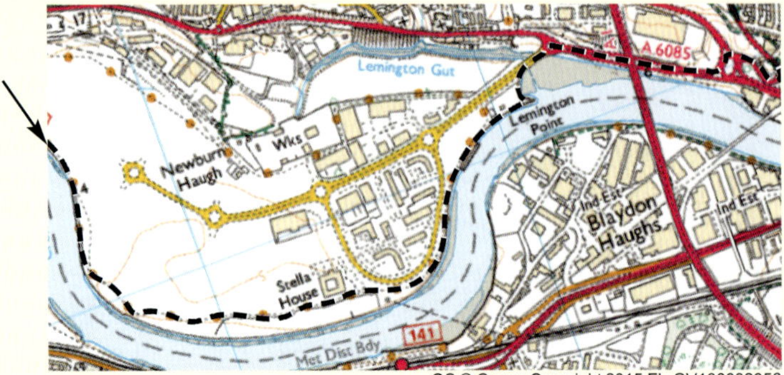

provides information about this section of the Tyne Riverside Country Park.

Eventually, you pass a pleasant green space with picnic benches where you may enjoy a short rest and enjoy the views. You may be able to watch members of the nearby rowing clubs honing their skills on the tidal waters of the Tyne. The river bears right and Newburn Bridge comes into sight. You pass a children's play area and some exercise machines (should you need them!) and the path bears left at a large concrete sculpture. You might like to puzzle out its meaning or just ignore it! Turn right to pass the top of the slipway, unless you wish to seek nourishment in Hedley's Riverside Café Shop or The Keelman pub to the right, then left, of the café.

The path continues around a car park, beside which is a monument to the Battle of Newburn Ford of 1640 when the victorious Scottish army gained access to Newcastle via this once-fordable river crossing. Several information panels provide details. The path makes its way across a small footbridge as the Reigh Burn enters the Tyne. Turn right and walk ahead to join an access road.

River God Tyne

You pass the Tyne Rowing Club (1852) on the wall of which is the sculptured representation of the River God Tyne. The three-stranded beard is taken to represent the three courses of the Tyne and the head-top basket appropriately shows coal and fish. The River Tyne was one of seven English rivers depicted in god-like form on the front of Somerset House in London (1786).

On the opposite bank is Tyne United Rowing Club and beyond the bridge, Newcastle University Rowing Club. The strong presence of these clubs serves as a reminder of how important rowing was on the Tyne in the 19th century when thousands lined the banksides to watch world champion oarsmen such as Harry Clasper and James Renforth. You pass The Boathouse pub where, to the left of the entrance, there is a plaque with further information about George Stephenson, while, to the right, markings on the wall indicate some dramatic flood heights of the Tyne, particularly that of the Great Flood of 1771.

You arrive at some traffic lights and Newburn, with its amenities and bus services, lies to the left. Take great care to cross the road as the traffic flow is controlled by lights at each end of the bridge. Walk ahead a few yards and bear left. A Royal Bank of Scotland (RBS) milepost indicates 'Newcastle 5'. Proceed ahead for about ¼ mile to a National Cycleway sign and fork right in the direction 'Hadrian's Cycleway; Newcastle Quayside 6 via riverside'.

The path leads down to a road (Shelley Rd). Turn left and continue along the pavement through Newburn Industrial Estate. Businesses here range from car dismantlers, to bread making, to 'Breakfast at Tiffany's' café. Relief comes when you arrive at the end of the road, at the edge of a field, at the sign 'Newburn Riverside ½; Newcastle Quayside 5'. Ahead, to the left, you may be able to see the brick cone of the former Lemington Glassworks (1787-1997), a listed building. There are further views of this reminder of local industrial heritage as you proceed.

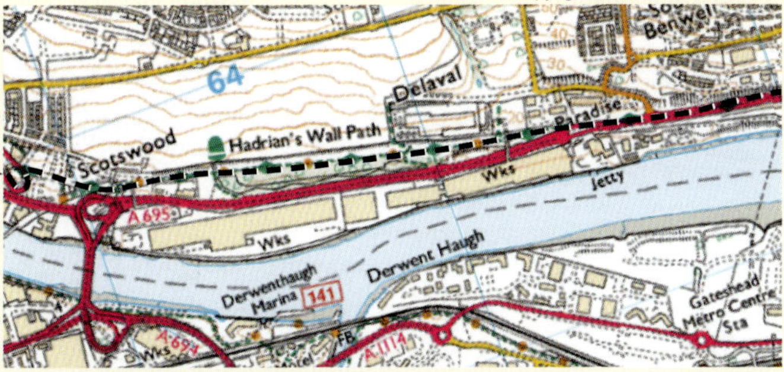

Turn right, walk along the path and you soon return to a wide expanse of river opposite a modern housing estate. Now simply keep to the riverside path and enjoy the views as you proceed through Newburn Riverside Park.

Newburn Riverside Park

This area has been reclaimed from its former industrial use. Until the mid-1990s it was dominated by the Stella North Power Station which was supplied by coal which arrived at substantial railway sidings. In addition there was a graphite plant. A twin power station, Stella South, stood on the opposite side of the river. The site was cleared by the year 2000 and an extensive business park, which you will pass, was constructed. The name 'Stella' came from the former Stella Hall estate, on the south side of the river, which had a long history dating from the 12th century when it was the site of a convent. The Hall was demolished in the 1950s.

Eventually, beyond the tree-lined path, a large office block becomes visible, currently occupied by the NHS, and, not surprisingly because of its location, called Stella House. You then see several other office blocks. Across the river, scrap metal begins to blot the landscape. However, if you are in need of refreshments, shortly after passing a pylon, watch out for a short path on your left leading towards blocks C & D Services. Turn right, walk about 75yds and cross over to Feel Good Food (weekdays only). Otherwise continue ahead. Below on the right is a small marina at Lemington Gut.

You arrive at an access road to the business park. Turn right, walk ahead and cross Lemington Bridge with its ornate white lampposts. Blaydon Bridge (1990), carrying the A1 over the Tyne, lies ahead, beyond which is the redundant

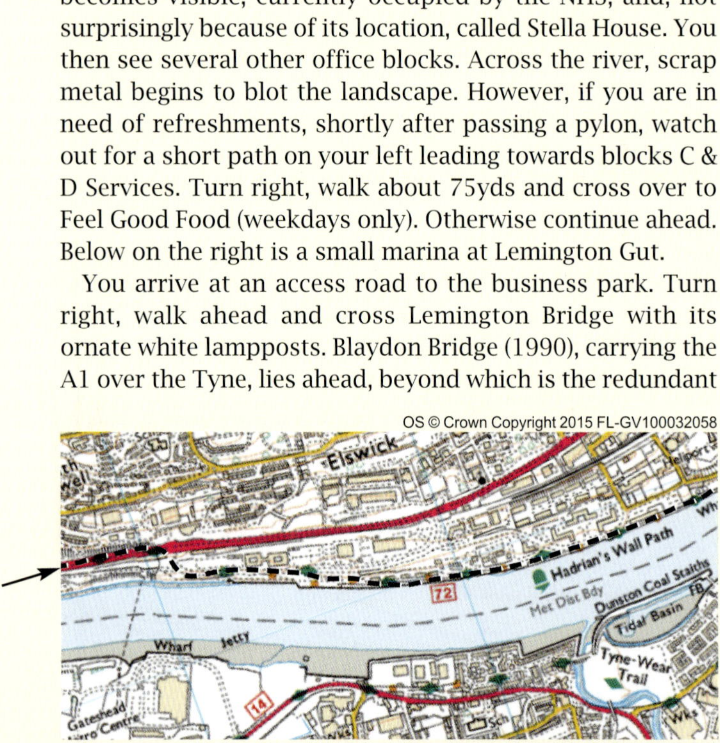

Scotswood Rail Bridge (1871) which formerly served the Newcastle to Carlisle Railway.

Bear right and join the riverside path. You pass a RBS milepost 'Newcastle 3¼'. Continuing ahead, with B&Q to the left, you reach a set of traffic lights at an access road. Turn right to walk a short distance along the riverside path to the entrance to Enterprise rent-a-car. Turn left up the narrow path and turn right. After a few yards, at the 'Cycleway 72' sign, use the pedestrian lights to cross the busy dual carriageway. Turn right and after some 150yds bear left to climb up the path on the Hadrian's Cycleway.

At the top of the rise, ignore a path off to the left but stop and look back over the grassy area to the left where you may be able to see a sculpture of white figures and a horse. This monument is a poignant reminder that coalfields were worked in this area until the late 1950s and it commemorates the death of thirty-eight miners at the Montagu View Pit in 1925. If you look across to the right, you can see the Scotswood Road Bridge (1967).

Miners' Memorial *(Photograph: Graeme Peacock)*

Walk ahead and at a fork bear left to continue along Hadrian's Way. Keep on the broad path. You are walking on land reclaimed from the crowded terraces that once ran towards the industries that lined Scotswood Road and the riverside. (Later you will pass an information panel that illustrates the significance of Scotswood Road in the Tyneside anthem *The Blaydon Races.*) You pass some remains of the abutments of the railway that once ran along here. Through the trees to the right, you will see a factory building. Until recently BAE Systems produced armoured vehicles here (in 2013 it was acquired by the north-east Reece Group). However, previously, for over 150 years, it was part of the site of the engineering firm, W.G. Armstrong and Company founded by William (later Lord) Armstrong.

Continue along the path. You may not realise it but you are walking through 'Paradise'! (An explanation awaits you later). Eventually the path descends to Scotswood Road. Continue ahead on the shared path and then use the traffic lights to turn right and cross over the dual carriageway. Turn left and proceed ahead. You pass two information panels: one tells of 'Paradise', the other of 'The Blaydon Races', although you may question if the panel is the right way round!

Lord Armstong

William Armstrong (1810-1900), having initially been a partner in a Newcastle Law Practice, subsequently devoted himself to engineering. He invented the world's first efficient hydraulic crane in 1847 and founded his Elswick engineering works which eventually stretched for over two miles along Scotwood Road. The company at first specialised in hydraulic machines and the Swing Bridge, which you will pass later, is still driven by its hydraulic engines. The company gained a world-wide reputation for armaments, including the construction of naval vessels for the Japanese. It was of vital importance during and after World War II and its armoured vehicles have been exported all over the world. His original company went through a series of mergers until it became known as Vickers Armstrong in 1927. In addition to his business activities he was a noted benefactor and he is particularly remembered for presenting Newcastle with land for Armstrong Park in Heaton and for Jesmond Dene. He was created Baron Armstrong of Cragside in 1887.

Now turn right down William Armstrong Drive. Cross over an access road and after some 40yds go down the steps on the right to join the riverside path at the Newcastle Business Park. You will follow this path for the next 2½ miles all the way to the Newcastle Quayside. If you look ahead diagonally to the right, on the skyline you may be able to see Anthony Gormley's iconic *Angel of the North* sculpture.

You come to 'The Hydraulic Crane', the first of a series of information panels detailing Lord Armstrong's engineering works and the industrial heritage of the Scotswood-Elswick area. You pass a number of public art works which may test your imagination and there are benches from which you can admire the developments taking place on the other side of the river. Look out in particular for the wooden loading jetty, the Dunston Staithes, a further reminder of the former importance of the river to the coal trade. The wide expanse of mud flats at low tide in this area enables you to appreciate the tidal nature of the River Tyne.

Behind the information panel, 'Armstrong's Works', is a vestige of the machine shop in the form of the arched arcade. You pass a small parade of shops. Eventually you come to the end of the Business Park and the bridges gradually come into view – all seven! Proceed ahead under the most recent version of the Redheugh Road Bridge (1983), the King Edward VII Rail Bridge (1906) and the blue Queen Elizabeth II Metro Bridge (1980).

Just before the Copthorne Hotel (1993), one of the earliest of the redevelopments in this part of the riverside, there is an information panel, unfortunately rather faded, 'Cleaning up the Tyne'. However, you may be able to discern for yourself that the Tyne has been restored, from being a conduit for sewage, to a regenerated source of joy to fishermen and, of course, to walkers!

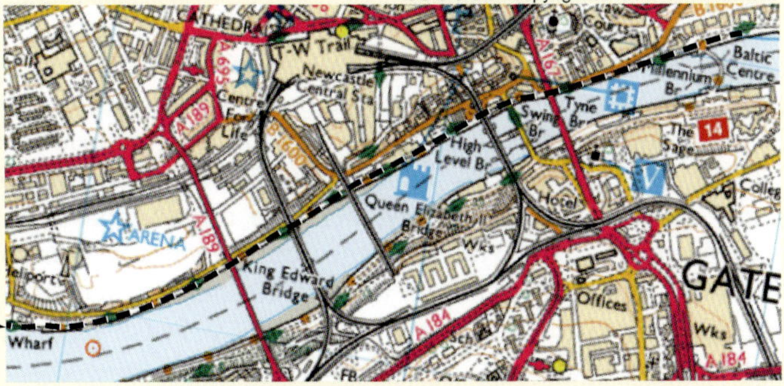

Seven bridges ahead *(Photograph: Graeme Peacock)*

Continue under the oldest of the current bridges, the High Level Bridge (1849), designed by Robert Stephenson. It still serves for motor vehicles on the lower deck and trains on the upper deck. You pass a nightclub which now occupies the former Fish Market (1880) with its roof-top sculptures of two fishwives and Neptune. Walk beneath the access road to the Swing Bridge (1876). On the left is the Guildhall, the centre of local government from the 17th century until 1858. It is used on ceremonial occasions, for example, by the Freemen of the city, and it contains some office accommodation.

Finally the trail leads beneath the Tyne Bridge (1928). Across the river you will recognise The Sage (2004), Gateshead's emblematic concert hall and music centre, together with the Baltic Centre for Contemporary Art (2002). The River Tyne marks the boundary between Newcastle and Gateshead, now, for promotional purposes, under the umbrella-title **NewcastleGateshead**. As you walk along the Newcastle Quayside, you pass the fine facades of some former business premises and the Customs House (1776). The much more modern Law Courts of 1990, an early contribution to the regeneration of the Quayside, appear on the left. You pass the John Wesley Memorial Fountain and at last you are at the Gateshead Millennium Bridge where this stage of the Daft as a Brush Cancer Patient Care Walk ends.

NewcastleGateshead

'NewcastleGateshead' is a fairly recent concept which arises from the need to present a joint case for culture, business and tourism. Their stories began at least 1900 years ago. Early settlements were probably established under Roman rule. Roman coins and artefacts have been found on both banks of the Tyne. In the 2nd century, near the site of the present Swing Bridge, a bridge, called Pons Aelius to honour the family name of Emperor Hadrian, was built. Later a fort, also called Pons Aelius, was constructed.

In the 6th century, following the Romans' earlier withdrawal from Britain, Northumbria, the northern-most of a number of independent Anglo-Saxon kingdoms, came into being. Here the spread of Christianity resulted in the development of monastic settlements. Bede refers to Utta as Abbot of Gateshead in 653. An Anglo-Saxon cemetery, presumed to be Christian, was built on the site of the Pons Aelius fort.

Following the Norman invasion, Gateshead and Newcastle gradually developed into substantial boroughs. Newcastle had a Royal Charter while Gateshead was within the domain of the Bishops of Durham. The early predominance of the coal trade was, from the 18th century, complemented by other industrial development. Both towns experienced increases in population. Like other industrial towns, there was a great deal of poor housing and inadequate working conditions. However, local industrial Victorian grandees built impressive properties in suburban locations such as Low Fell and Jesmond.

By the end of the 20th century, the area's traditional heavy industries had all but disappeared. Government action and local initiatives have resulted in a shift to modern light and high-tech industries, as well as recognition of the importance of commerce, retailing, leisure and tourism. Newcastle has two universities and, like Gateshead, a well-established higher education college. Regeneration schemes have completely changed the character of the town centres and both sides of the river.

Today's visitors can enjoy many historic buildings in Newcastle, including two cathedrals and the 12th century castle keep and, in Gateshead, its iconic Baltic and Sage arts centres and Millennium Bridge.

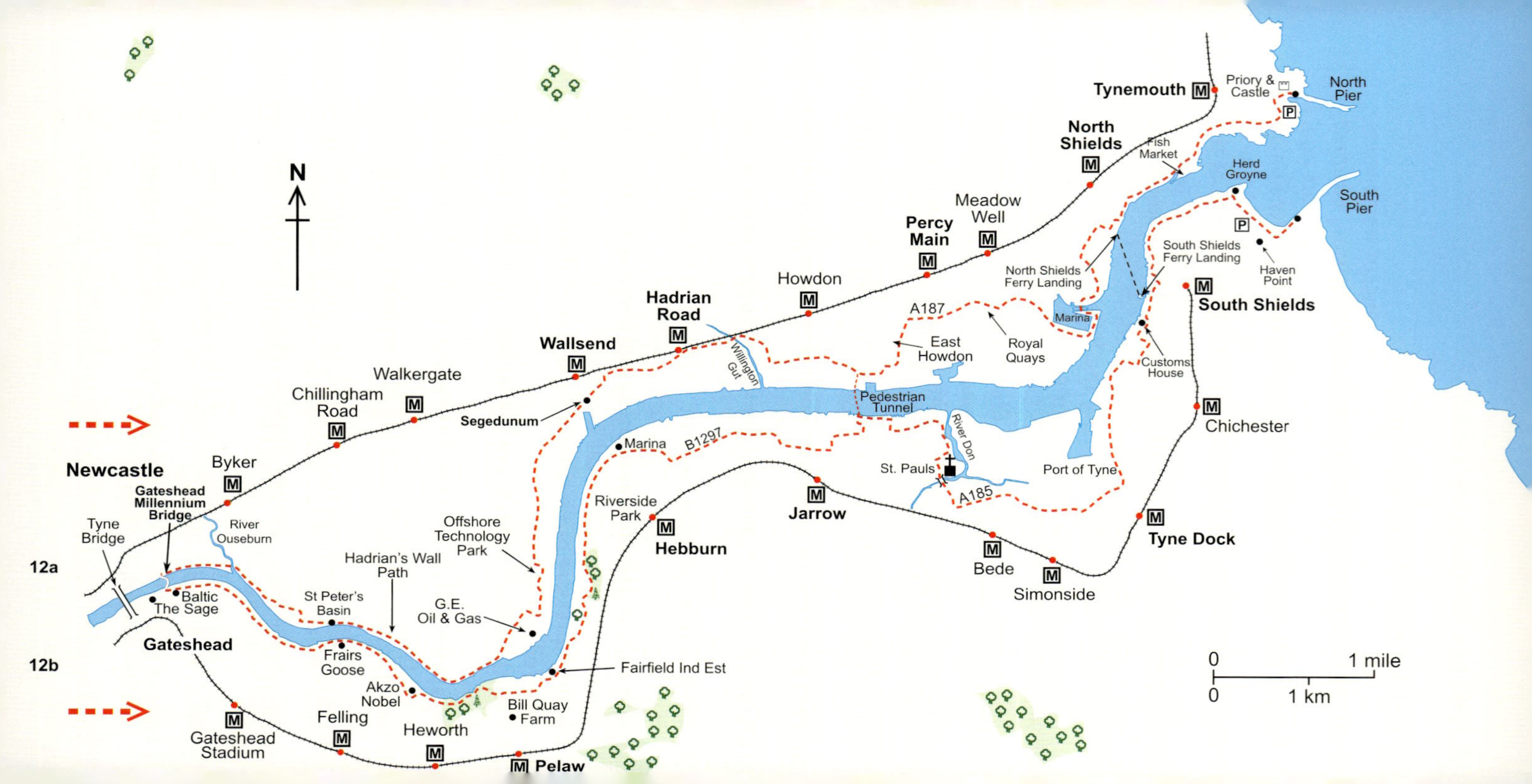

N
Tynemouth
Priory & Castle
North Pier
North Shields
Fish Market
Herd Groyne
South Pier
Meadow Well
Percy Main
Howdon
Hadrian Road
Wallsend
Walkergate
Chillingham Road
Byker
Newcastle
Gateshead Millennium Bridge
Tyne Bridge
River Ouseburn
Segedunum
Willington Gut
North Shields Ferry Landing
South Shields Ferry Landing
Haven Point
South Shields
A187
Royal Quays
East Howdon
Marina
Pedestrian Tunnel
River Don
Customs House
Chichester
St. Pauls
Port of Tyne
A185
Marina
B1297
Riverside Park
Jarrow
Hebburn
Bede
Simonside
Tyne Dock
Offshore Technology Park
Hadrian's Wall Path
St Peter's Basin
G.E. Oil & Gas
Baltic
The Sage
Gateshead
Frairs Goose
Akzo Nobel
Fairfield Ind Est
Bill Quay Farm
Felling
Heworth
Pelaw
Gateshead Stadium
12a
12b
0
1 mile
0
1 km

STAGE 12
NewcastleGateshead to the sea
13½ miles (21.7km)*

Choice of routes

As the River Tyne finally makes its way to the sea, long-distance walkers have the choice of completing the trail by walking down the north side of the river to Tynemouth or down the south side to South Shields. Day-walkers, of course, could enjoy both experiences! The existence of a pedestrian tunnel and a ferry service also make it possible to experience both sides by crossing from one side of the river to the other during the journey to the sea. The proximity of Metro stations and bus stops means that, with numerous entry/exit points, this stage can be easily sub-divided to suit individual needs. The two routes are set out separately below as **12(a)** and **12(b)**; both include reference to their respective entry/exits points and river crossing opportunities. *The distances covered will vary depending upon which route/combination is followed.

The route is along surfaced paths and pavements with several short climbs. Inevitably, as this is now clearly an urban environment, the river, at times, is hidden from view and the trail needs to follow busy roadside pavements. Due care needs to be taken when crossing all roads. Many of the pavements are shared with cyclists and on occasions there is a degree of uncertainty about the designated lanes to use, so again attention and awareness are required. There are no more bridge-crossings but with the addition on this stage of the pedestrian/cycle tunnel, twin vehicular tunnels, and a ferry, the total number of river crossings throughout the trail comes to eighty-two.

12(a) The north side of the river to Tynemouth

Direct route 12½ miles (20.1km)

(For **12(b)** The south side of the river to South Shields see Page 171).

The trail begins on the Newcastle Quayside at the Gateshead Millennium Bridge. Initially, the riverside path passes modern offices, dwellings and a marina. It eventually leads through the important offshore technology park, which has replaced the former Walker shipyards. It follows an old railway line and passes Wallsend, the site of the Roman fort of Segedunum, as well as the former world-renowned Swan Hunter shipyard. The trail reaches the Tyne Pedestrian and CycleTunnels which provide an opportunity to cross to the south side of the river should you wish. A further few miles lead to the Royal Quays shopping outlet, a marina and the Port of Tyne International Passenger Terminal. From here, there is a short steady climb before the trail descends to the North Shields ferry landing. Once again there is the opportunity of making a river crossing. The route to Tynemouth, however, continues ahead past the North Shields Fish Quay and along a lengthy promenade. The trail ends with a further short climb before the descent to the sea and the north pier at Tynemouth. There are numerous signs throughout the trail for Cycleway 72/Hadrian's Way which you will generally follow – but not always!

Entry/exit points	**Newcastle and Gateshead Quaysides GR257640); Metro Stations at Wallsend 5½ miles (8.8km); Hadrian Road 6 miles (9.7km); Percy Main 8¼ miles (13.2km); North Shields 11 miles (17.7km); Tynemouth 13 miles (20.9km)**
Maps	**OS Explorer 316 Newcastle upon Tyne; Tyne & Wear A-Z Street Atlas**
Refreshments	**Newcastle and Gateshead Quaysides; Royal Quays; North Shields Fish Quay; Tynemouth village centre**

The walk

You start from the Newcastle side of the Gateshead Millennium Bridge, the world's first tilting bridge, which came into use in 2001 before being officially opened by HM The Queen in May 2002. On your left is the Malmaison Hotel, which has retained part of the façade of the original Cooperative Society Ltd building (1889).

Walk ahead along the quayside passing the Pitcher and Piano pub, the golden-globe topped sculpture *Swirle Pavilion* (Raf Fulcher, 1998) with its impressive list of ports associated with the Tyne's earlier shipping trade, the jetty

The Swirle
(Photograph: Graeme Peacock)

for River Escape Cruises and the tall conical *Blacksmith Needle* (British Association of Blacksmiths Artists, 1996). You pass impressive-looking office blocks and modern apartments. In the tree-line, above the only green space that manages to survive at the moment, is St Ann's Church (1764-8), built with stone from the demolished quayside section of the Town Wall.

After about ½ mile, you reach the confluence of the rivers Tyne and Ouseburn. On the left is one of the thousand mileposts, erected by the Royal Bank of Scotland, to commemorate the creation of the National Cycle Network. You will pass more of these. On the right, a few yards further, an information panel tells some of the story of the Ouseburn. To the left, above a road bridge, is the tall chimney of the former Maynards Toffee Factory (1906). This was converted into contemporary office space in 2010 after lying derelict for more than twenty years.

Follow the path as it bears left to exit onto a road. Turn sharp right and proceed ahead, crossing a bridge, to arrive at the east side of the River Ouseburn. The Ouseburn Barrage (2009) on the left is designed to control the water

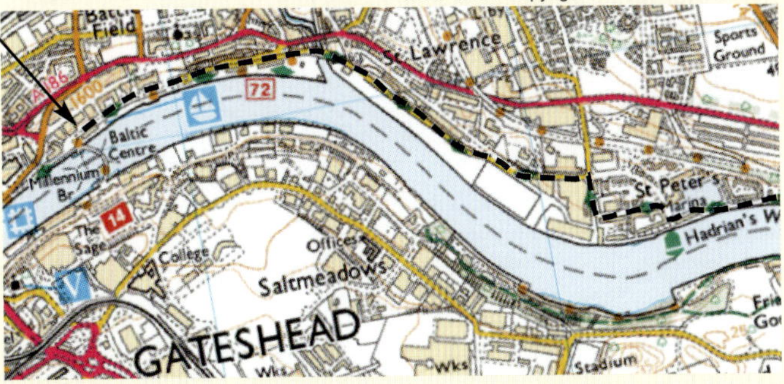

level in the Ouseburn, while a few yards away is The Tyne Bar, a noted watering hole! On the right is the Hub cycle shop and café with an outdoor seating area from where there are fine river views. An information panel, 'Spiller's Car Park', provides details of the many interesting buildings in the vicinity.

The riverside path lies invitingly ahead and is a popular spot for anglers. (At the time of writing its use is permissive, courtesy of Newcastle City Council, and, should the path be closed for any reason, you would need to follow the narrow pavement on the left-hand side of the road). As you walk along the quayside, you may see a notice advising that there is no exit ahead for pedestrians and cyclists. However, at the end of the paved riverside path, before reaching some stone bollards, you need to turn left and make your way across the car park to a small gate in the metal fence. Exit through the gate, cross the road with care, turn right and proceed ahead on the narrow pavement to a junction. Near this point, on the quayside, once stood the 120ft (36.5m) tall, Spiller's Flour Mill, a noted local landmark until its demolition in 2011.

Notice on your left, the artwork, *Spiller's Forest* (Nick James, 2005), created from redundant quayside timbers salvaged from the former Spiller's Wharf, which was located nearby. Cross the junction with care and continue ahead, bearing left. Follow the road, using the pavement on the right-hand side. You pass between the British Engines/Bel Valves works and arrive at a crossroads. Turn right and walk down towards the river. After about 100yds, look out for a sign for Hadrian's Way.

Turn left and continue along the road (Bottlehouses Street) to enter an area of modern housing (St Peter's Basin).

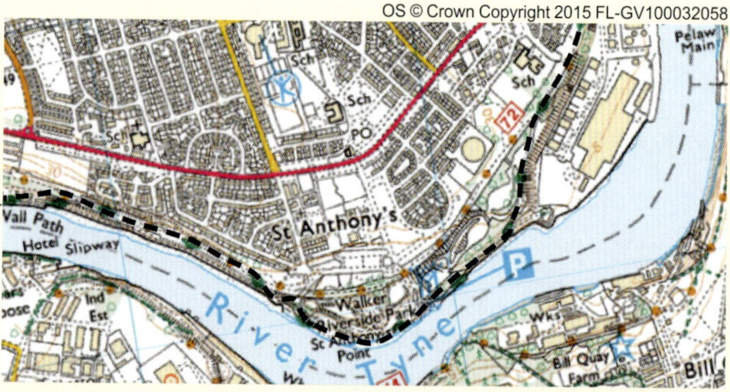

St Peter's Basin Marina *(Photograph: Graeme Peacock)*

Turn right, just before the Bascule Bar & Bistro and the marina. Walk towards the riverside and at Chandlers Quay, almost hidden in the bushes on your left, is the foundation stone laid in 1989 by the then Prime Minister, Margaret Thatcher. Across the river, to the right, you should be able to see the floodlights of Gateshead International Stadium. Turn left and continue ahead. Before you cross the bridge at the Marina Office, you might like to stop and admire some fishing vessels in the marina, details of which are on an adjacent information panel. Once safely across the access bridge, simply follow the pavement as it continues along the riverside. When you come to the end of the housing you join a surfaced path which you will follow for the next 1¼ miles.

As you stroll ahead, on the opposite side of the river, you will see the small Friars Goose marina. You might be surprised to see the first of two green poles standing guard in the river but these are navigation beacons which are illuminated at night. Ignore paths and road off, as the trail keeps close to the riverside. On the other side of the river you will see the large Azko Nobel industrial complex (previously British International Paints). You pass an information panel with details of the former St Anthony's Lead Works, responsible for considerable riverside pollution – ahead, there are still a few warning notices!

Keep on the riverside path which at one point leads up a short flight of steps. Eventually, you arrive at a fork in the path, at a brick wall with three inset seating spaces. Bear left on the same metalled path you have been following, as it leaves the riverside. At the top of the short rise, turn left and then almost immediately right (here you leave the C72 Hadrian's Way). Follow the path with the perimeter fence on your right as it descends to an access road (Wincomblee Road) at the entrance to GE Oil and Gas (formerly Wellstream International). Turn left and proceed ahead on the right-handside pavement past various other offshore-subsea industry companies.

Offshore-subsea industry

The Walker riverside, once dominated by shipbuilding which included the important Walker Naval Yard opened in 1912 by Armstrong Whitworth, is now home to Shepherds Offshore Technology Park. A significant number of specialist engineering and design companies are engaged in producing key elements of the subsea infrastructure industry. You can marvel at the two yellow cranes, affectionately known locally as 'David' and 'Goliath' which are used to load the huge pipe and cable-bearing reels onto appropriate sea going vessels.

Turn left, after about ½ mile, and walk about 75yds up Malaya Drive (named after the battleship launched in the former Walker Naval Yard in 1915). Now turn right in the direction, 'Cycleway 72, Wallsend 1½, Tynemouth 7'. For the next 2 miles or so, the track follows the line of an old railway. From time to time, there are glimpses of the river as it stretches ahead. After crossing a second bridge, on your right, through the trees, you will see part of the former Wincomblee Workshops of White Street.

At one point, in the absence of the bridge, the path descends to cross a road (Welbeck Road) before climbing back on the other side to pass some renovated post- World War ll prefab housing. The path descends again to cross

Wincomblee Workshops

This once fine Edwardian building, opened in 1915, is believed to have been Armstrong Whitworth & Company's Shipyard Apprentice School, converted in more recent years into office and workshop accommodation and boarded-up following a fire in 2010. The adjacent road is named after the early shipbuilder Charles Mitchell (1820-1895). Mitchell like Joseph Whitworth was an associate of William Armstrong and their two companies had likewise merged earlier.

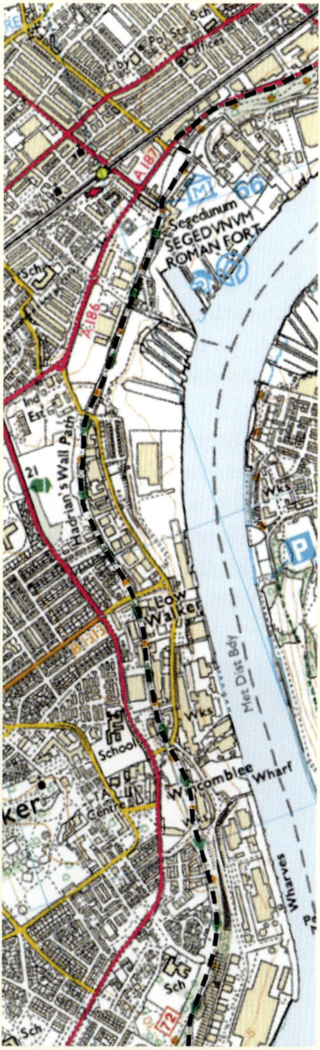

another road. On the buttresses of the old railway bridge there are emblematic reminders of the significance of the Emperor Hadrian Augustus to this area, as you approach his 'wall's end'. You may notice the prominence of the name 'Hadrian' as you proceed! Cross the road and climb back to continue along the track. On the other side of the river you should be able to see the landmark, tall spire of St Andrew's Church (redundant) at Hebburn. This was provided in 1872 by Andrew Leslie who established what was to become, as Hawthorn Leslie, a major shipbuilding company until its demise in 1982 – a reminder of the earlier dominance of shipyards on both sides of the Tyne.

After going under a road bridge you reach an information panel about waggonways. (For good views of the river and the site of the former Swan Hunter shipyard (see below) you might like to walk down the path on the right for some 25yds.) Continuing ahead you soon come across a white building on the left, a reconstruction of the bath house at the Roman fort of Segedunum at aptly named Wallsend.

On crossing a small bridge, to the right you will see the entrance to the former shipyard of Swan Hunter. A few yards further, a ramp on the left leads to an access road from

Segedunum

The fort was built to defend the eastern end of Hadrian's Wall. Its present-day museum tells the story of Wallsend's Roman past to its modern industrial heritage of which the observation tower affords good views. Touch-screen computers provide an opportunity to pursue your own interactive discoveries. The reconstructed bath house building is based on the baths at the fort at Chesters which you passed on Stage 4 of the trail. Visitors are welcome to use the café and gift shop. Nearby, Wallsend Metro Station even has some signs translated into Latin!

Segedunum Fort *(Photograph: Graeme Peacock)*

where, if you wish, you can visit Segedunum or walk a further ¼ mile to Wallsend Metro Station.

Swan Hunter

The yard was responsible from about 1860 until 2007 for building a large number of important passenger ships, naval ships and oil tankers for many nations. It provided a major source of local employment, for example, having some 11,000 workers when it was nationalised in 1977. Its eventual closure was a major blow for the whole area. Swan Hunter Design and Engineering Office is the only operative vestige of this once famous company.

As he indicates in the Foreword to this guidebook, international rock star Sting was born and bred in sight of the huge tankers which were launched at Swan Hunter's shipyard at the bottom of his street. He has drawn on his roots in Wallsend to write about the demise of a shipyard, in a musical, *The Last Ship,* which was premiered to great acclaim in 2014. Earlier Sting commissioned a painting by the American artist Stephen Hannock, *Northern City Renaissance: Newcastle, England.* Exhibited in the Laing Art Gallery in 2008 and 2012, the painting sets out to celebrate the regeneration of the Tyne following the closure of the shipyards and coalmines.

The closure of Swan Hunter's Neptune Yard was movingly highlighted in the song *Big River* by Jimmy Nail in 1995. This is one of several songs about the Tyne which include the beautiful early 18th century ballad *Waters of Tyne* which tells of a plea to a boatman to ferry a lover across the river. Sting and Jimmy Nail have been among the many artists to record this song.

After passing Segedunum, a sign indicates 'Hadrian's Cycleway 72; Royal Quays 3 ½; North Shields 5'. Continue ahead on the metalled path to cross an access road and further cycleway signs. From time to time you continue to catch glimpses of the river. After about ½ mile you reach a red archway marked 'National Cycleway Network – Hadrian's Cycleway 72' and the end of the metalled path. Proceed ahead along the shared cycle/pedestrian pavement. Cross Davy Bank and turn left to cross the road to follow the cycleway sign 'Tynemouth 72'. Turn right and continue along the pavement next to the A187 (Hadrian Road) for about ½ mile.

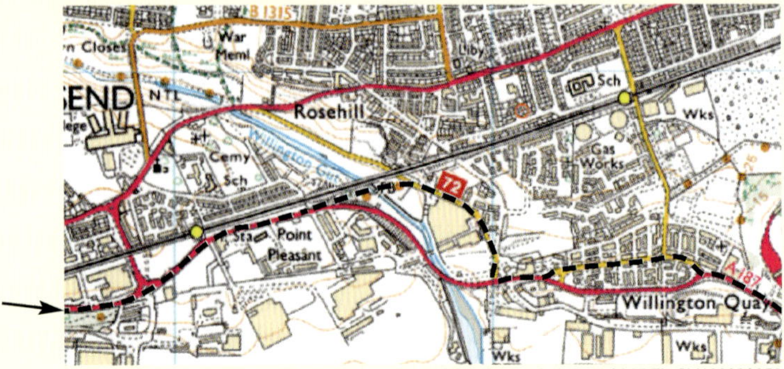

In a short while, you pass an entrance to Hadrian Road Metro Station – a possible escape route for a weary walker! You pass a Fire Station on your right. Later a sign tells you that you are on your way to Willington Quay and North Shields. Bear left and take the right-hand fork through the trees, hopefully leaving the left-hand path for cyclists! As the path descends, on the left, you should see the imposing Willington Viaduct, originally part of the Newcastle to North Shields Railway of 1839, now carrying the Metro line. A metal bridge leads over the Willington Gut (earlier the Wallsend Burn) which flows into the Tyne via the small Willington Quay Marina. The path then crosses through a pleasant grassy area where you may hear and see Metro trains as they thunder over the viaduct. You join a minor road and bear right to follow the 'Cycleway72 Tynemouth' sign. On the right, you pass Bridon, the successor of the early 19th century Hood Haggies rope works (which had become part of British Ropes in 1959).

Continue along the pavement to follow the road as it bears right past the Albion Inn on your left. You return to the main road (Hadrian Road). Turn left, walk straight ahead to pass the Jet Filling Station and the 'Welcome to Willington Quay' sign and proceed along the minor road (Bewicke Road). As you walk along the left-hand side pavement look out, immediately after Carlyle Street, for a foundation stone laid by Lord Warkworth (Duke of Northumberland) on the wall of the Willington Quay Social Club. You might notice there are two other foundation stones and look out for some inset memorial stones further ahead! Continue ahead as Bewicke Road eventually bears right towards a roundabout to rejoin Hadrian Road.

Continue on the left-hand pavement and go across Cumberland Street, where there is a sign to St Paul's Centre and Church. After a few yards, turn right at the small 'Tyne Cycle & Ped Tunnel' sign and use the traffic island to cross the main road with care. Walk ahead and turn left to follow the railings on your right, through which you will regain views of the river. On the left, you should see the tall office building housing TT2 (the operating and management company of the Tyne Tunnels since 2007) and a Tyne Tunnel ventilation tower. You soon reach an information panel that provides details of the North Tyneside Waggonways. Just beyond this is the access road that leads to the Tyne Pedestrian and Cycle Tunnels. The Grade II Listed tunnel opened in 1951, pre-dating the road tunnel by 16 years and serving as a vital link for thousands of shipyard workers on both sides of the river.

Here you have the opportunity, should you wish, to cross the river and continue down the south side. If so, as you walk down the access road to the pedestrian tunnel, you pass an information panel about George Stephenson the so called "father of the railways", who lived and worked for a time near here. Also notice the two sculptures by Fiona Gray, *Echo* and *The ones that got away* (2004). Information about the tunnel can be found at both the entrance and exit. See Page 179 for details of the walk from the tunnel exit on the south side of the river.

The tunnel is expected to re-open in June 2015 after major refurbishment, however, should this not be the case a free shuttle-bus replacement service operates. The bus stop is a short distance east of the tunnel entrance.

Not far now

Continuing down the north side of the river, on the left you will see the colourful public art work *Gateway to the Coast* (Lynda Nelson, 2011). On the right you may get a glimpse of the river before the path bears left past a sign indicating a number of routes ahead. As the path rises, you pass Ristorante Sambuca, formerly a dockland pub, the Duke of Wellington. A few steps ahead on a grassy slope is a small metal sculpture *Subway to the south* (Fiona Grey, 2011) inscribed with place names such as Rotterdam, Murmansk, Panama City and Vancouver. Would these be the likely destinations for tunnel users?

Turn right (note that Cycleway 72 continues straight ahead at this point), walk along Lesbury Street past a children's play area and then turn left into Chatton Street. You are now in what has become the small enclave of East Howdon, effectively cut off from Howdon itself by the tunnel approach roads. Proceed, using the ample grass verge if appropriate, to the end of what is now Baird Avenue. Walk ahead at the sign 'Safer Routes to School' and follow the surfaced path which leads through an underpass brightly adorned with bold graffiti (this is a legal art site and an example of the good work of the Phoenix Detached Youth Project in this area).

Ahead you can see evidence of a railway line and at weekends, further up the line, you may even glimpse a train! A waggonway carrying coal down to the riverside staithes ran here from the mid-18th century. Later it became part of the vast network of steam driven waggonways from the numerous local coalmines. Trains, operated by volunteer enthusiasts, now run on the North Tyneside Steam Railway on the 2 mile journey from the Stephenson Railway Museum close to Percy Main Metro Station.

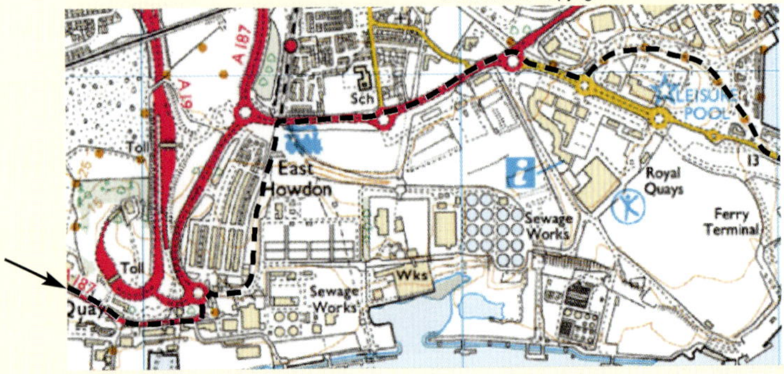

To continue from the underpass, turn sharp right and follow the ramp up to the main (A187) road again. Cross at the pedestrian lights, turn left to walk ahead on the shared path for the next ½ mile. You pass a roundabout (the road to the left leads to Percy Main Metro Station in about ¼ mile). Look out for a sign indicating that North Shields is 2.6 kms. (Perhaps the unusual use of metric numbers is for the benefit of visitors from other parts of Europe!) Continue ahead and at the next roundabout leave the A187 to take the second road on your right. Walk down Coble Dene. On your right is the Royal Quays Outlet Centre (1966) where, amid the fifty or so retail outlets, you are sure to find a cup of coffee and more after walking some 8¾ miles.

However, to continue the walk, proceed to the pedestrian lights. Turn left, cross Coble Dene, walk ahead a few yards and turn right onto the Hadrian's Cycleway. You may be heartened by the sign indicating the distances, 'Shields Ferry 1½ miles; North Shields Fish Quay 2¼ miles; Tynemouth 3 miles' - although the end of the walk is actually a little further! Follow the path as it gently winds its way down towards the river through the pleasant Redburn Dene Park. This provides another fine example of the regeneration of much of the riverside. Here the industrial past, of what was once a route from the coal mines to the river, has been transformed as a 'Rugged

Reclaimed parkland

Landscape', with reclaimed timber staithes appearing to stand guard amid large boulders along the way.

Ignore paths off and carry on in the direction 'Cycleway 72' until you arrive at a road. Cross the road and proceed ahead in the direction indicated by the 'Cycleways C2C, 10 & 72' sign. Ahead you might see evidence of a cruise liner or one of the North Sea ferries which dock at the Port of Tyne International Passenger Terminal. The path leads down to the Royal Quays Marina. The cycleway turns left here but the trail bears to the right to go around the marina in an anti-clockwise direction. An information panel, two-thirds along the first side of the marina, provides interesting details of what was once the Albert Edward Dock (formerly Coble Dene Dock).

You soon get close to the riverside where there may be larger sea vessels temporarily moored. You pass the *Earl of Zetland*, a permanently moored bar/restaurant and functions facility. A red metal sculpture, *Tyne Anew* (Mark di Suvero, 1999) stands on the corner. It is said to reflect the industrial foundation and future of Tyneside but you may need to work that out for yourself. As you make for your exit point on the permissive path, you pass what looks like a clock tower. This is in fact the former Accumulator Tower, now a listed building, installed in 1882 to operate the lock gates.

Turn right, just before the Royal Quays Marina reception building, to follow across the permissive walkways over the

Royal Quays Marina

docks. Warning lights will alert you to any temporary closures. If the lock is in the process of filling, walk a little further to a second walkway (in the very unlikely event of both walkways being closed for a long time, you would need to retrace your steps to the entrance to the marina and follow the cycleway route). Once across the walkways, continue straight ahead along the path with the grassy area on your right. At the time of writing, there was no access on the pathway immediately on the right across the site of what was once Smith's Dock.

Smith's Dock

This one-time shipbuilding area, initiated by Thomas Smith in the 1850s, was later to concentrate more on ship repair work as Smith's expanded its building interests more in the Tees at South Bank. It finally closed around 1990 and then, like others of its type, the dockland became a neglected eyesore. However, since 2007 a multi-million pound clean-up has prepared the ground quite literally for a major regeneration programme which will involve housing, hotel accommodation, shops and cafés. Pedestrian access will then certainly enhance this route along the Tyne.

Turn right onto the pavement and follow the road as it climbs steadily. At the top of the rise, bear right to follow Cycleway 72. You should be able to get some fine glimpses of the river. You may see the passenger ferry plying between the North and South Shields ferry landings. Ahead on the left, the two white towers are the former navigational aids High Light and Low Light. The structure jutting out on the other side of the river is South Tyneside College's Marine Safety Training Centre and Fire Training Centre especially for personnel involved in the offshore industries.

You descend to a road junction where, at the time of writing, the road ahead was closed. Hopefully it may not be too long before there is direct access from here to the North Shields ferry landing. In the meantime you need to turn left, continue 150yds or so and then turn right to follow the signs for Cycleway 10(E). You pass the Lawson Street business units and the road descends to a T-junction at the end of the street. Turn right and follow the road as it climbs to the left. Walk up some steps to Tennyson Terrace and turn immediately right. After a further 100yds, turn right at a metal sign to leave the road and walk between the fencing. Go down a short flight of steps and almost immediately take the steps (some 50!) on the left, or follow the ramp, to descend to a road. The ferry landing is almost opposite.

Here you have the last opportunity to cross the river should you wish to end the walk at South Shields. Whichever route you choose, it is well worthwhile adding a short ferry journey (there and back if appropriate) to your River Tyne experiences. The crossing only takes 10 minutes and the ferry leaves every half-hour. To continue down the south side of the river see Page 185.

To resume the trail towards Tynemouth, continue ahead with the ferry landing on your right and an information panel on your left. This panel is part of the North Shields Heritage Trail (panel number 1 is at the ferry landing) and, unless you are in a great hurry, it is well worth looking at each one. You will certainly learn a lot about North Shields but it is up to you to spot them! The properties on the left-hand side have been converted into residential apartments. A plaque on the last building indicates that this was originally the Sailors' Home (1856). Walk ahead, with care, over Borough Road to the information panel on the corner.

Proceed ahead with The Porthole pub on your right and cross over to this side of the road when convenient. Fine apartments on both sides of the road have replaced what was

High and Low Lights

once a densely packed area around a former dry dock and engineering works. You will see a replica of the 'Wooden Dolly' outside the Prince of Wales Tavern (Old Wooden Dolly). An information panel provides an explanation. As you continue ahead, you will see a white tower on the left, the High Light, a former navigational aid. Shortly afterwards, its counterpart, the Low Light, appears ahead as you reach a tall, blue-grey corrugated building, the former ice factory.

In a few paces you arrive at the west end of the North Shields Fish Quay where there is a further information panel. Now follow the quay. On your left, you will find a miscellany of premises and on your right, perhaps some fishermen repairing their nets before you reach the small fleet of boats at the end of the quay. Follow the left-hand side pavement past further restaurants and cafés where fish is obviously the dish of the day!

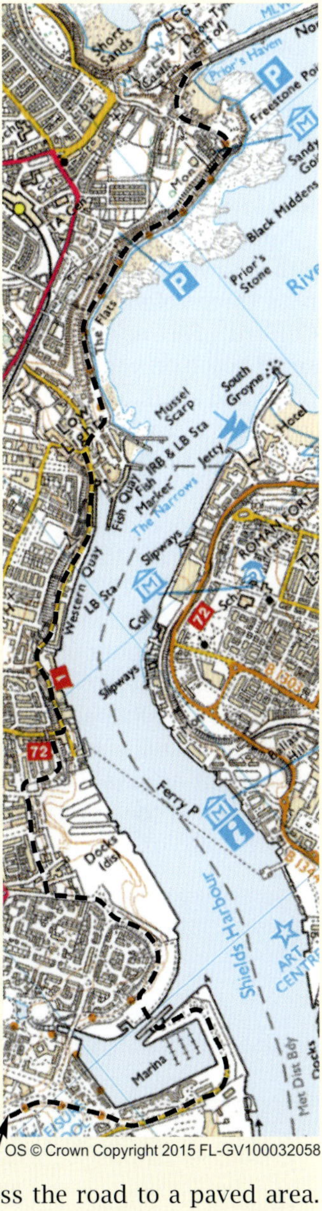

Just before the road bears left, after the Aroma Coffee shop, with Vita House ahead on the right, turn right to cross the road to a paved area. Walk about 20 yards and turn right again. On your left, you pass the former Dock Master's House and the Fishermen's Mission with its ornate balcony. At the end of the Mission building, turn left onto a paved path. As you proceed ahead the Low Light (to be converted into a heritage centre) is on your right and on your left are the remains of Clifford's Fort

(1692); unfortunately the relevant information panel lies a few hundred yards ahead. Follow the wall of the fort and after a sharp left-hand bend, cross the road to walk up the ramp to join the riverside path. As the path bears left, notice on your right the remains of the Lloyds Jetty, the site of the former hailing station from which vessels were hailed for Lloyds insurance purposes.

Now, at last, the mouth of the Tyne comes fully into view, although you still have some way to walk! Proceed ahead to pass three colourfully-restored navigation buoys and the Clifford's Fort information panel on your left, as well as a small beach on your right. Ahead are splendid views of the north and south piers. On the opposite side of the river, you will see a riverside wall, Herd Groyne, with its red lighthouse built in 1882 at the mouth of the Tyne before the piers were constructed. It still acts as a navigational aid.

As you proceed along the promenade, towering above on the bankside are the Sir James Knott Memorial Flats which were built in the 1930s, funded by the Sir James Knott Trust in memory of the wealthy shipowner of that name. They were originally built with seafaring families in mind and were among the first to incorporate design features to minimize possible air raid damage. Inevitably the eye is drawn to the tall and imposing monument dedicated to the memory of Admiral Lord Collingwood (1748-1810), one of the heroes of the naval Battle of Trafalgar (1805). You will find details on the relevant information panel as you

Sea ahead at former hailing station

proceed ahead. You soon reach a further information panel 'Shipwrecks and Heroes' which illustrates the perils once faced by shipping and the importance of the piers that lie ahead. The notorious Black Midden rocks are recalled on a small plaque on the railings a short distance ahead.

Just before the end of the riverside path, you pass a National Cycle Network sign. The path then ascends quite steeply, passing a further sign indicating the end of the C2C cycle route. At the top of the rise, the headland on the right is known as the Spanish Battery. It is said that this is so-called because from here Spanish mercenaries manned cannons to defend the castle and the Tyne in the 16th century. You join a road and on your left is Tynemouth's Volunteer Life Brigade's Watch House and Museum. Ahead, on the cliff top, stand Tynemouth Priory and Castle (English Heritage). Below, on the right, are Tynemouth Rowing Club and Tynemouth Sailing Club.

English Heritage flies the flag atTynemouth

Walk ahead and go over the small bridge. **Tynemouth** village lies ahead up the steep bank with its Metro Station about ½ mile away. However, to complete the walk you need to turn right here at the 'Welcome to North Pier' sign. Continue down the path where, a short distance beyond the green space on the left, a very welcoming marker stone announces that you have reached the end of the Daft as a Brush Cancer Patient Care Walk!! However, if the pier gates are open, and you are really in the mood, you may wish to add an extra ½ mile and proceed to the end of the pier (and, of course, walk a further ½ mile back!). Whatever you choose to do, you deserve to receive hearty congratulations. Well done!

Tynemouth

Beautiful beaches and sandy bays, together with the historic ruins of the priory and castle, make Tynemouth a sure-fire destination for holidaymakers and day visitors. Surfing is now firmly established as an addition to the attractions of swimming and building sand castles on Tynemouth's Longsands beach. Tynemouth is also a popular place to live, within easy commuting distance to Newcastle and Gateshead. Its Victorian railway station, now a stop on the Tyne and Wear Metro, hosts a comprehensive arts and crafts market every Saturday and Sunday. Tynemouth Village, centred round Front Street, boasts an eclectic collection of shops with some in a former church as well as many pubs, cafés and restaurants. Other attractions include the Blue Reef Aquarium, Tynemouth Park, near the Longsands beach, with lots of attractions for children, and the magnificent statue to Admiral Lord Collingwood which overlooks the Tyne. The Metro station is about ½ mile from the pier.

End in sight

12(b) The south side of the river to South Shields

Direct route: 13½ miles (21.7km)

The trail begins in Baltic Square at the south end of the Gateshead Millennium Bridge next to the Baltic Centre for Contemporary Art and close to The Sage Concert Hall. After a short initial section, the trail joins a pleasant riverside path. It leads past a small marina before detouring around an important industrial site. It then passes through a riverside park, an impressive example of the reclamation work which has taken place on the south side of the river. There are splendid views of the new industries that have regenerated the north side of the river. You reach the entrance to the Tyne Pedestrian and Cycle Tunnels which you could use to cross to the other side of the river. Continuing along the south side of the river, the trail goes past an important 7th century monastic site, goes near the former Roman fort of Arbeia, and passes the modern Port of Tyne facilities. There is a further possible river crossing at the South Shields ferry landing. Finally the trail passes some modern riverside properties and a recently renovated promenade as the Tyne reaches the sea at South Shields pier.

Entry/exit points	Newcastle and Gateshead Quaysides (GR257640); Metro stations at Pelaw 3¾ miles (6km); Hebburn 5¼ miles (8.2km); Jarrow 7½ miles (12km); Tyne Dock 10 miles (16km); South Shields 14 miles (22.5km)
Maps	OS Explorer 316 Newcastle upon Tyne; Tyne & Wear A-Z Street Atlas
Refreshments	Newcastle and Gateshead Quaysides; Friars Goose Marina; The Customs House, South Shields; Littlehaven, Haven Point, cafés and restaurants in South Shields centre

The Walk

From Baltic Square at the south end of the Gateshead Millennium Bridge, walk ahead to the left of the Baltic Centre for Contemporary Art. Turn right at the bollards before Jury's Inn and then left to join the road (South Shore

Iconic bridge

Road). A sign indicates you are on Cycleway 14. There are many further signs telling you that you are on Cycleway 14 and that you are heading to the Ped (Pedestrian) Tunnel and South Shields, as well as being on the Keelman's Way. Helpful as the signs might be, don't rely too much on these indications as from time to time your route will deviate from them.

Continue straight ahead along South Shore Road passing a miscellaneous collection of workshops and business premises that unfortunately impede views of the river. However, after about ½ mile you catch a brief glimpse of the Tyne just before you turn right at Lafarge Aggregates. Walk uphill for about 50yds and turn left at a cycleway sign. You pass a further number of industrial sites and

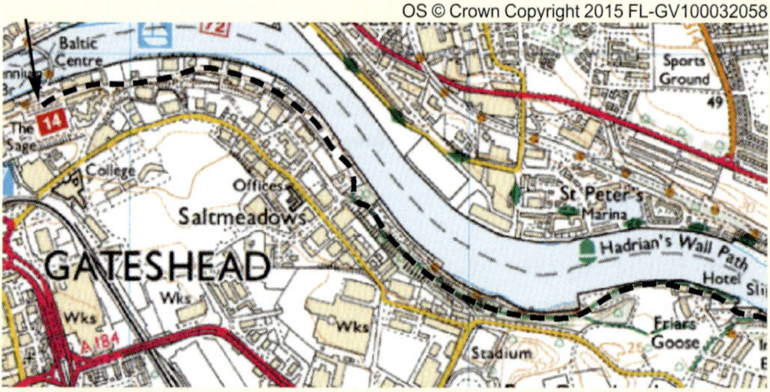

workshops before the road eventually descends to the riverside with a pleasant sweep of the Tyne ahead.

Here, you will find an information panel about the adjacent Kittiwake Tower which was caringly erected by Gateshead Council when the birds were displaced from their previous nesting site in 2002, following the redevelopment of the Baltic Flour Mills into a contemporary arts centre. The panel helps to identify this colony of gulls.

Turn left at the next set of bollards and go down a flight of steps. (Alternatively you can keep straight ahead on a higher path for about 300yds until the paths converge near a car park.) Proceed along the riverside path. You walk through a car park and immediately turn left.

(However, if you are ready for refreshments post-midday, you could continue straight ahead and climb some 150yards to The Schooner which claims to be "the 2nd best pub in Gateshead"!)

Proceed to a junction, where you turn left downhill to continue on Cycleway 14 along the pleasant riverside path. The path affords good views across the river and you will be able to identify the modern housing and marina at St Peter's Basin. You reach some apartments as the road climbs steeply between them and the oddly named Elephant on the Tyne Hotel, Bar and Bistro. On the left, beyond the hotel, is the small Friars Goose Marina, while on the right you will find an anchor resting on a stone.

Friars Goose Marina

A plaque, beneath the anchor monument, explains that this area, like many you will encounter on your journey down the Tyne, has been reclaimed from former heavy industrial usages. It was in the local coal mines that Thomas Hepburn was instrumental in establishing the Northern Union of Pitmen in the 1830s and, near here, the so-called 'Battle of Friars Goose' took place in 1832, when the colliery owners enlisted the army's support in quelling striking miners.

After about 75yds, as the road bears right, turn left and then go immediately right to follow the cycleway. The surfaced path climbs slowly between the trees. Care needs to be taken to look out for cyclists, particularly at bends and narrow sections. The path leads to a more open space where you may find horses grazing. Eventually, below, you

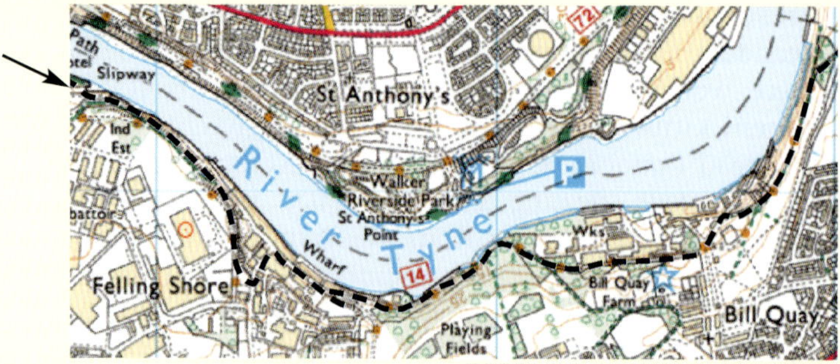

see the rooftops of the Akzo Nobel industrial plant. You lose sight of the river for a while as the path diverts around the plant and joins an access road. Turn left and follow the road as it turns right at the entrance to the site. The International Paints Division and a major research and development unit of the world-wide company of Akzo Nobel are located here. With over 900 employees, it is the largest private sector employer in Gateshead.

Follow the road as it climbs steadily for a few hundred yards, then turn left at a cycleway sign into Abbotsford Road where there are light industrial premises. Continue for about 125yds and make sure not to miss the narrow path on the left, just before KGM Refrigeration and opposite Tuffnells Parcels Express loading bays. Pass between the metal barriers and go down the path with the Akzo Nobel complex on your left and then housing on your right. You arrive at an access road with corrugated fencing on your right, behind which are stables. Cross the road and go between the bollards to rejoin the cycleway at the riverside. The industrial buildings are soon left behind and the river returns into view. The path undulates and at the top of the rise, by looking back, you get an idea of the size of the Akzo Nobel plant.

Continue ahead along the undulating path. After a while you lose sight of the river and you reach a path off to the right. However, carry straight on here, unless you wish to visit Bill Quay Community Farm or go to Pelaw Metro Station (as indicated on the other side of the sign on the left of the path). The farm, a few hundred yards up on your right, was established in 1986 on reclaimed land with the aim of increasing awareness of farming and gardening within an urban area, particularly with young people in mind. Pelaw Metro Station is about ½ mile beyond the farm.

Continue ahead with a high wall on the left, while on the

right you may catch glimpses of the farm. You reach an access road to the Fairfield Industrial Park. This was once part of the thriving dock area of Bill Quay. Cross the road to continue ahead on the Keelman's Way and cycle route. To your right is The Cricketers pub. The path bears left, beside a grassy area, and then right, as it climbs between the trees. On the other side of the river, you will begin to notice how shipbuilding and its related industries at Walker have been replaced by more modern offshore industries. The riverside becomes dominated by huge pipe-carrying reels. As you advance further there is more evidence of the growing significance of the subsea industry. Look out for the two yellow loading cranes affectionately known locally as David and Goliath, and the tall Technip building at the Shepherd Off-shore Technology Park.

David and Goliath (*Photograph: Graeme Peacock*)

At a junction, follow the cycleway to the left to enter South Tyneside. The river comes back into view. As you proceed ahead, you may hear and see Metro trains passing to and from South Shields. The path reaches a junction after a bollard. Turn left and descend to the riverside to meet an access road which you follow to the right. Hebburn Riverside Park on your right provides yet another example of reclamation from the heavy industrial sites that once dominated this area. You may see a line of small boats moored close to the bankside as you approach an information panel on the right with details of the public art work *Flash@Hebburn*.

You arrive at a boardwalk-jetty with convenient benches and a car park, a favourite spot for fishermen. The wrought iron art work in the railings was designed by local school children and you might enjoy identifying their representations of local scenes, water, earth and air. At the end of the boardwalk an information panel tells of local industrial and social heritage. On the other side of the river, you should be able to pick out the observation tower on the site of the Roman fort of Segedunum, just above the site of the former Swan Hunter shipyard (see Page 159).

Follow the road for about 250yds, passing Hebburn Marina and Boat Club, before turning left at the NCR 14 sign 'South Shields-Pedestrian Tunnel-Jarrow'. (If required, Hebburn Metro Station is about ¼ miles further up the road - Prince Consort Road.) Continue along the path for a few hundred yards passing the 'TS Kelly Sea Cadets' premises (HMS Kelly being a famous destroyer built at the Hawthorn Leslie shipyard, the site of which you will see shortly). Bear left to descend once more to a riverside path and some pleasant modern housing. From the end of the path, the remains of the Swan Hunter shipyard, together with the Segedunum observation tower, are now more clearly visible. Follow the road as it climbs past the boarded-up former **Hawthorn Leslie shipyard**.

Standing out ahead is the exceedingly tall spire of St Andrew's Presbyterian/URC Church which Andrew Leslie provided for Hebburn in 1872. However, the church as such became redundant about 40 years ago and has been put to various charitable uses, even with plans to convert it from church to brewery! Next to the church is its former school, restored in 1985, currently South Tyneside Social Care and Health Directorate.

Hawthorn Leslie shipyard

The shipyard was created by Andrew Leslie who came to Hebburn from Aberdeen in 1853. Many of his workforce, who lived in adjoining company-built housing, were from north-east Scotland, so earning the area the nickname 'Little Aberdeen'. In 1886, after Leslie's retirement, the company merged with R & W Hawthorn, locomotive and engine makers, to become Hawthorn Leslie. The yard produced a wide range of vessels, including warships, passenger ships and oil tankers, before closing in 1982.

Further up, on the right-hand side of the road, the information panel 'Little Aberdeen' gives information about some of the ships built here.

A short distance further up the road you arrive at the T-junction (Lyon Street) where you turn left. The river now remains out of sight and you need to be prepared for about 1½ miles of roadside walking until you reach Jarrow. Follow the busy straight road (B1297), the name of which changes after the first roundabout from Lyon Street to Wagonway Road. Happily, in contrast to signs of dereliction, you will see some activity as you pass the entrance to A&P ship repairs, conversion, marine and energy services. In 1995 A&P acquired what had been at one time part of **Palmer's Shipbuilding and Iron Company**.

When you reach Windmill Way roundabout, ahead you should be able to see the tall ventilation shaft of the Tyne Tunnel. There is an information panel 'Old King Coal'. This provides a strong reminder of the hardships and the dangers endured by miners and their families.

Carry straight on as the road becomes Blackett Street and then Western Road. Eventually, you arrive at a roundabout

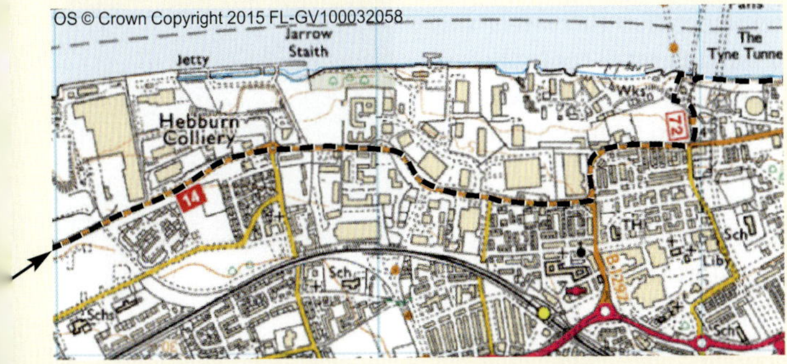

Palmer's Shipbuilding and Iron Company

(Sir) Charles Mark Palmer (1822-1907) set up a very successful shipbuilding business in 1851 in what was at that time the small mining village of Jarrow. The area's claim to fame had already been laid as nearby-St Paul's monastery was home to the Venerable Bede (673-735), monk and historian. Many centuries later, Palmer's shipyards, steel works and related industries led to a huge growth in Jarrow's employment and population. Where Andrew Leslie established 'Little Aberdeen', Charles Palmer created 'Little Ireland' as Tyneside's Irish community expanded. Unfortunately the closure of the shipyard and other local industries in the mid-1930s had a devastating impact, with unemployment rising to some 75% of the local workforce. Consequently Jarrow rose to national prominence when, in 1936, some 200 men walked nearly 300 miles to London on the 'Jarrow Crusade' to carry a petition seeking remedy to the high level of unemployment and poverty.

near the centre of Jarrow. If you wish to seek refreshments or you feel you have come far enough after walking about 7 miles, turn right for local amenities and Jarrow Metro Station.

However, to continue on the trail, use the traffic island to cross straight ahead and go down Ormonde Street. Until recently, the pub to the right was The Jarrow Crusaders with its sign recalling the 1936 march to London. As you continue along Ormonde Street, you pass the splendid 1920s façade of what was once one of the Montague Burton stores. This serves as a reminder that this street was a thriving retail centre before shops were replaced by houses and commerce moved elsewhere. You may just be able to make out the company logo 'The Tailor of Taste'. The store closed in the 1960s and is currently occupied by Balmoral Interiors.

Walking for jobs

At the end of the street turn left, walk down past the ventilation tower to reach a busy road. Use the traffic island to cross over and continue ahead for about 100yds. The entrance to the Tyne Pedestrian and Cycle Tunnels lies to the left. The Grade II Listed tunnel opened in 1951, pre-dating the road tunnel by 16 years and serving for many years as a vital link for thousands of shipyard workers on both sides of the river.

Here you have the opportunity, should you wish, to walk beneath the river and continue the trail down the north side of the Tyne. Information about the tunnel can be found at both the entrance and exit. See Page 162 for details of the walk from the tunnel exit on the north side of the river. The tunnel is expected to re-open in June 2015 after major refurbishment, however, should this not be the case a free shuttle-bus replacement service operates. The bus stop is a short distance east of the tunnel entrance.

Otherwise, to proceed down the south side of the river, walk ahead and follow the ramp to the riverside. Walk along the riverside path where at last you can enjoy good views of the Tyne. On the opposite side of the river you should be able to see the ventilation tower and the approach roads to the vehicular tunnels above which you are now walking. Continue ahead to join an access road. Walk up the road with fencing on your left, beyond which is Cemex Aggregates Jarrow Wharf. At the end of the road you join the main road (Priory Road).

Turn left and walk about 150yds before turning left to follow the sign 'Tyne Dock 2 miles; South Shields 4 miles'.

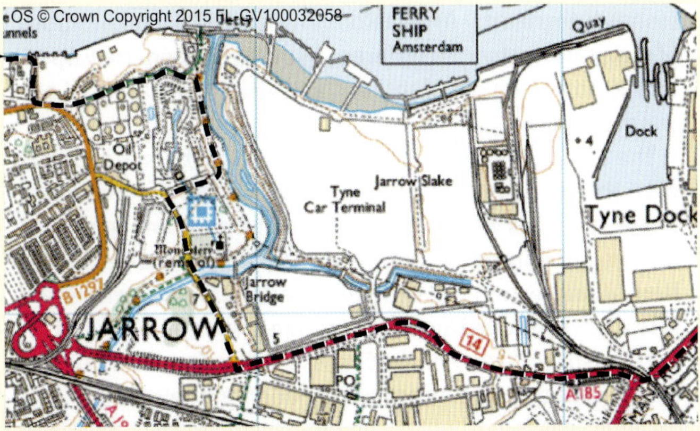

After a short distance, bear right past the bollards and follow the metalled path as it descends to an access road near the River Don. At the junction, bear slightly left to join the clear, but narrow, riverside path (otherwise, if the path looks very muddy you can continue along the access road). The path rejoins the road and you pass a car park area.

Follow the road as it turns right at some boulders. Time permitting, you then have a number of options. After about 100yds, on the left, you arrive at an entrance gate into the grounds of **St Paul's Church and Monastery**. This is an important site associated with the noted 7th century monk and historian, the Venerable Bede. Go through the gateway to visit the church and/or the site.

(Opposite, on the right-hand side of the road, a path leads through the parkland to 'Bede's World' with exhibitions and insights into the Venerable Bede and life in Saxon times (entrance charge applies). Next to the museum there is also a café at the 18th century Jarrow Hall.)

To proceed on the trail, continue ahead along the access road (or after visiting the church/site walk down the broad path from the main entrance to the church) and turn left at the main road (Church Bank). Proceed ahead. At the beginning of the bridge, there is an information panel about the old Jarrow Bridge, said to be part of a medieval route to the monastery. It is worth stopping to enjoy the view down the River Don to the old bridge. There's no pavement on

St Paul's Church and Monastery

Although the church has undergone many modifications over the years, it still has its late 7th century foundations, its Saxon chancel and its Norman Tower. There is evidence of stones from nearby Arbeia Roman fort as well as exhibitions of many artefacts from different periods. It is generally open, thanks to a team of volunteers, and visitors are assured of a warm welcome.

The adjacent monastic ruins are part of a twin monastery with that of St Peter's at Wearmouth, some 7 miles away. These two sites were among the most important centres of learning in Europe during the 7th and 8th centuries. It was here at Jarrow that the Venerable Bede (673-735), monk and historian, produced an eclectic range of works, including his *Ecclesiastical History of the English People.* Details of the site can be found on the information panels in the grounds.

this side of the road, however, you can take advantage of the generous grass verge. At the bottom of the road turn left and walk along the shared pedestrian/cycle path parallel to the road. Be prepared for the fact that the next 1¾ miles or so lead alongside the A185 and A194, through the busy industrial area of Tyne Dock, dominated by the Port of Tyne facilities.

You pass an information panel, 'Life and death on Jarra Slaks' which provides details of the local environment and its history. Proceed ahead past the Port of Tyne Jarrow Slake entrance with its important car terminal. After going beneath a bridge, there is a further panel with the rather grim title, 'Slime-dripping arches'. Here you will find information about the prolific writer **Catherine Cookson** as well as about Tyne Dock.

You arrive at a further entrance to the Port of Tyne at Tyne Dock. Cross the access road with care to pass

St Paul's Church and Monastery (*Photograph: Graeme Peacock*)

(Dame) Catherine Cookson

The author Catherine Cookson (1906-1998) was born and brought up in the Tyne Dock area of South Shields. She wrote more than 100 novels which have become extremely popular world-wide, many having been adapted for films and TV. They were mainly inspired by her unhappy childhood in a deprived environment. The strange title given to the information panel is in fact the name given by her to a series of bridges, one of which you have just passed under, and which were used to transport coal for shipment from the Tyne. She was a generous benefactor of many causes and her Foundation continues to support worthy endeavours. South Tyneside, rightly proud of her fame, used the name 'Catherine Cookson Country' for 25 years until 2012 when it was decided to attempt to broaden the appeal of the town with new signs indicating a range of attractions. However, the series of information panels around the town still bear the earlier brand name.

Navigation House. A sign indicates that Tyne Dock Metro Station is ¼ mile to the right. At the roundabout turn left in the direction 'Riverside B1302'. Look out for a bench behind which are three metal figures of local significance (Sarah Milligan, comedian; a Roman centurion and Norman Fry, cycle maker). Ignore the sign indicating 'New Route' to the right and instead keep to the left, with Kennedy's pub on the right (on the wall of which is 'Temple Town 1809'). The busy road then bears right and you pass Port of Tyne Logistics Service on the left, and on the right, the now inappropriately named Tyne View House.

Further on, as the road begins to rise, look out for the narrow opening at Readhead Landing where you can just catch a glimpse of the Tyne, at the site of the former Readhead Shipyard's West Docks. This was another of the major shipbuilders and later on the trail you will see a plaque (once located here) in memory of employees who died in World War I. Turn left, when the main road (Commercial Road) bears right at the top of the rise. Walk down the access road (West Holburn) where you are rewarded for the long trek through the industrial environment with views across a wide section of the river. Through the railings, you will see the **Port of Tyne** International Terminal and possibly one of the DFDS

Seaways vessels. Follow the road which, after the houses, turns right to re-join Commercial Road.

Turn left and then left again, immediately after the Trimmers Arms and Lobster Pot Restaurant. The road (Hill Street) bears right past the pleasant Rose and Crown pub (with the addition title of 'The Holburn' to distinguish it from another Rose and Crown!). From here there are good views of the river, the Royal Quays Marina (former Albert Edward Dock) and both the south and north ferry landings. Walk ahead and make your way past some boulders and through an area of old parking bays of the former Middle Dock.

Port of Tyne

In 1968 the Port of Tyne Authority replaced the Tyne Improvement Commission as the body responsible for port and navigation on the River Tyne along the 17 mile stretch of the river, from the Tide Stone near Wylam (which you walked past earlier), and for a further mile past the piers. It operates the cruise and North Sea ferry terminals, the Tyne Distribution Centre on the north side of the river for the import of VWs and the Tyne Car Terminal on the south side for the export of Nissans from the plant at Sunderland. Tyne Dock also deals with a variety of bulk cargo imports including a large amount of coal – this in marked contrast to the historical outward movement of coal from the Tyne!

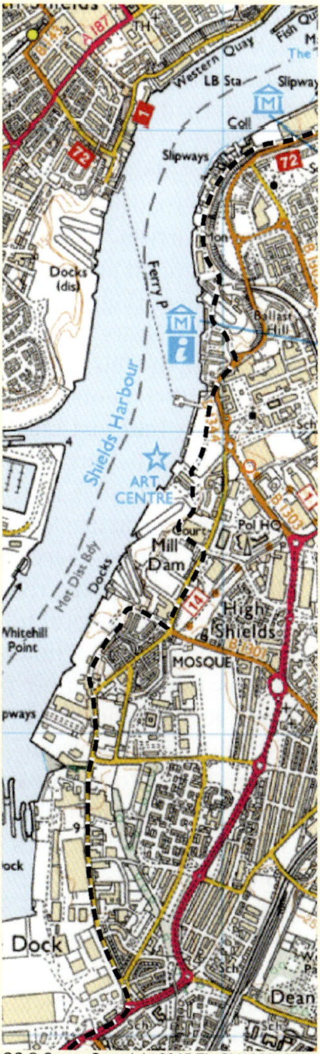

(There are plans for mixed-use redevelopment of this area which could lead eventually to the need to re-route part of the trail along Commercial Road.) The path bears right to the main road.

Turn left to re-join Commercial Road. On the right are South Tyneside Law Courts. After about 100yds, turn left to leave the roadside path. Walk down the narrow path and descend thirteen steps (to avoid the steps you could continue straight ahead) towards a housing complex. Keep to the left, ignoring the first road on your right, and follow the road as it bears right, then left. Look out for 2 bollards on the right, at which point you leave the road to turn left. Mill Dam (1865) is on the right. The name comes from the 13th century mill that once stood here. In a few paces you arrive at The Customs House, the former Board of Trade shipping office (1863), restored and extended in 1994 as an entertainment and arts centre. The Green Room bar-bistro-coffee shop is open every day.

Make your way to the riverside where there are excellent views. There is a helpful information panel with details of South Tyneside attractions. Facing the river, next to The Customs House and now private accommodation, is the former River Police and Tyne Port Sanitary Authority building of 1886. A plaque provides details.

From The Customs House walk ahead, past the poignant Merchant Navy memorial which recalls the large number of seamen who lost their lives in World War II. Some 75 yards further, a plaque on the promenade wall is dedicated to employees of Readhead's Shipyard who fell in The First World War. Continue along the neatly redeveloped riverside path and in a short distance you reach the South Shields ferry landing. South Shields pier and the end of the walk lies about 2¼ miles ahead.

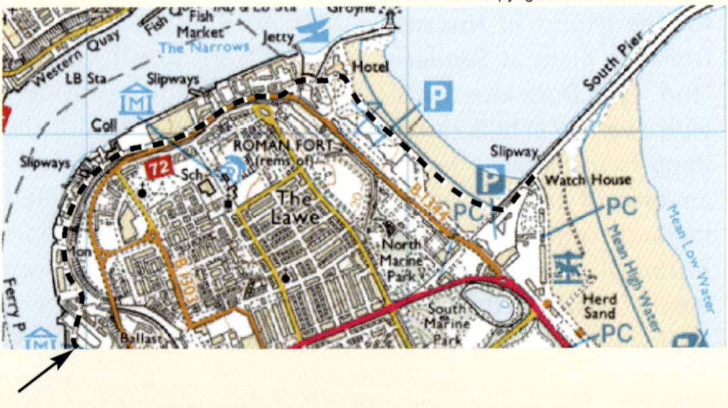

Merchant Navy memorial

Here you have the last opportunity to cross the river should you wish to end the walk at Tynemouth. Whichever route you choose, it is well worthwhile adding a short ferry journey to your River Tyne experiences (there and back if appropriate). The crossing only takes 10 minutes and the ferry leaves every half-hour. The ferry waiting room contains a comprehensive information panel which includes a history of the ferries as well as an overview of this stage of the trail. See Page 166 for details of the walk from the North Shields ferry landing.

To continue from the South Shields ferry landing, with the river on your left, walk along the riverside promenade now regenerated with modern dwellings replacing old industrial sites. You simply need to keep close to the riverside. You cross the walkway over a former dry dock and pass a flagpole with compass points marked in the stone surrounds. Just before a larger former dock, you'll find the welcome sight of a small damsel clutching a ship and waving

Ferries in sight

a greeting. However, she happens to be in the form of Irene Brown's sculpture *Spirit of South Shields* (1998).

A damsel beckons
(*Photograph: Graeme Peacock*)

The path very briefly joins the road. Here it is worth crossing to the other side of the road to see the extension of the dock where you may be surprised to find *Fleet*, a further art work by Irene Brown (2004). Here seven small stainless steel collier brigs recall the transport of coal down the Tyne. Walk a short way alongside the road then turn left, passing some modern office accommodation on your right. Continue downstream to the end of the riverside path where you reach a car park. Bear right to pass the South Shields Sea Cadets premises and make your way to the access road at Comical Corner, the strange name apparently reflecting rather awkward nearby river currents.

Turn left at the corner and continue ahead along what is now Wapping Street.

Wapping Street

Here wooden boats can be repaired and old craft carefully restored among the street's fascinating variety of marine businesses, boatyards and slipways, which include the North East Marine Trust with its Boomerang Boat Museum (open Tuesday, Wednesday and Saturday). At the same time the new focus on offshore industries is reflected in South Tyneside College's Marine Safety Training Centre and Fire Training Centre. There are several opportunities to catch glimpses of the Tyne and on the north side you should be able to pick out two tall white buildings, the High Light and the Low Light, that once served as navigational aids.

Wapping Street joins a main road (River Drive) at the bottom of a hill. You need to cross over the road, with care, to use the pavement on the other side. (Before you proceed you will notice some steps up the bankside. If you wish to detour to see or visit the Arbeia Roman Fort and Museum, climb these steps, walk a few paces ahead and turn left into a car park area. From here, there are good views of the reconstructed fort built in AD160 to guard the entrance to the Tyne. Should you wish to visit the fort, follow the path around the school playing field.)

To continue, walk along the right-hand pavement, and then cross back to the other side of the road again when the pavement resumes on the left. Soon there is further evidence of regeneration as modern housing comes into view. Turn left at the access road into the attractive properties of Harbour View. Follow the road as it bears left and then right to arrive via a few steps to a further riverside promenade. Turn right and walk along the promenade where you can enjoy the good views across to the North Shields Fish Quay, the 1930s James Knott Memorial Flats towering above on the bankside, the Priory and Castle at Tynemouth and the tall and imposing monument dedicated to the memory of Admiral Lord Collingwood, hero of the naval Battle of Trafalgar (1805).

Across the Tyne from Herd Groyne (*Photograph: Graeme Peacock*)

Follow the path which turns inland and at the end of the railings, go down the steps and walk the short distance across the tiny bay to reach a riverside path where you turn left. (Alternatively, if the tide has covered the beach, follow the access road ahead to the main road. Turn left past South Shields Sailing Club and then after about 100 yards turn left and make sure to double-back immediately through a car park to pass the Simonside Centre for Positive Youth Activity to pick up the riverside path with the tiny beach on your left.)

Proceed along the path as it hugs the riverside with The Little Haven Hotel on the right. At a junction, you reach a panel with historical details of the North and South piers and the Herd Groyne. A few yards ahead, along the groyne or riverside wall, is the Port of Tyne's Herd Groyne Lighthouse which has acted as a navigational aid since 1882, nearly thirty years before the two piers ahead were completed.

However, to continue on the trail you need to turn right at the information panel and follow the path, with the hotel on your right. You walk through the artwork *Conversation Piece* by the Spanish sculptor Juan Muñoz (1999). At the last count there were twenty-two figures engrossed in conversation! Bear left to climb a short set of steps that lead to the result of another regeneration project: Littlehaven promenade, seawall and coastal park (April, 2014).

Follow the promenade around the bay. There are several good photo-opportunities to capture the mouth of the river and the twin piers. A set of steps leads to an upper walkway and the sculpture *Eye* (Stephen Broadbent, 2014). However, continuing along the promenade you pass a series of 'portholes' before arriving at *Sail*, a further work, with a viewing circle, by the same artist. The tall modern building to the right is Haven Point (2013) leisure facility which includes a visitor centre and café.

You now need to walk along the pier for about 400yds, passing Watch House, the headquarters of South Shields Volunteer Life Brigade (founded 1866), to the marker stone indicating the official end of the Daft as a Brush Cancer Patient Care Walk. However, if the pier gates further ahead are open, and you are really in the mood, you may wish to add just under a mile and proceed to the end of the pier (but remember you'll have to walk back!). Whatever you choose to do, you deserve to receive hearty congratulations. Well done!

South Shields

With a population of over 80,000 South Shields is the largest town in South Tyneside. Following the demise of traditional shipbuilding and mining, services and tourism now provide important inputs into the local economy. The Port of Tyne Authority is headquartered in South Shields and provides an important source of employment. Its activities include car exports from Nissan and, somewhat ironically, import of coal!

South Shields has six miles of beaches, including The Leas, finishing point of the annual Great North Run. It also has two attractive parks, North Marine and South Marine, from the former of which there are splendid views of the mouth of the Tyne. The site of the second century Roman fort of Arbeia with its reconstruction of a Roman Gatehouse, its museum and excavations is an important tourist attraction. Catherine Cookson is remembered in the South Shields Museum and Art Gallery. Near the museum, the statue of John Simpson Kirkpatrick is a poignant reminder of a hero of the First World War who died at Gallipoli. The Metro station is about ½ mile from the pier.

The River Tyne finally reaches the sea
(photograph: *by kind permission of Airfotos: www.airfotos.co.uk*)

APPENDIX I
Getting to the sources and from the finish

Information about public transport and taxi services should be confirmed directly with service providers.

To the sources

Both sources are located in isolated spots in sparsely-populated landscapes. To get to the sources you will need to use your own transport or a combination of public transport and taxis. Alternatively many walkers make use of two cars, parking one at either end of their walk. Hexham provides an important link between both the North and South Tyne with bus and rail services as well as several taxi firms.

Source of the North Tyne

Own transport

If you are arranging to be dropped off by an accommodating relative or friend, to reach the North Tyne source you need to leave the B6320 at Bellingham and follow the C200 through Kielder Village for about three miles. The trail starts just before the England/Scotland border about 475 yds beyond Deadwater Farm. There is limited roadside parking space.

Public transport

You can travel from Newcastle to Hexham either by bus or by train. Arriva bus number 685 departs from Eldon Square bus station Newcastle. Northern rail trains to Hexham depart from Newcastle Central Station. From Hexham Bus Station, Howard Snaith Coaches and Tyne Valley Coaches run services to Bellingham, Mondays to Saturdays. The Howard Snaith Coaches carry on to Kielder Castle twice a day. There is no public transport from Kielder to the start at Deadwater. For taxis consult Tourist Information Centres (see Appendix II).

Source of the South Tyne

Whether you travel by your own or public transport, you can only use vehicles to a point which lies two miles from the source, i.e. you have to walk two miles before reaching the Trail starting point.

Own transport

Take the B6277 from Alston and follow the signs to Garrigill. Go through Garrigill, bear left at a junction and carry straight on when the Pennine Way road goes off to the right. After about two miles, you come to the end of vehicular access at a cattle grid. You must now walk to the source along the bridleway.

Public transport

You can travel from Newcastle to Haltwhistle either by bus or by train. Arriva bus number 685 departs from Eldon Square bus station Newcastle. Northern Rail trains to Haltwhistle depart from Newcastle Central Station. Wrights Brothers Coaches bus number 888 operates a once a day service from Newcastle Coach Station to Alston during July, August and September. For taxis consult Tourist Information Centres (see Appendix II).

From the finishing points

From Tynemouth Pier

Retrace your steps to the main path and turn right to reach Front Street. Turn left and walk ahead to Tynemouth Metro Station (½ mile).

From South Shields Pier

Retrace your steps to the main road, cross over at the lights and walk ahead, passing Haven Point leisure facility on your right and continue straight ahead to South Shields Metro Station (½ mile), or South Shields Ferry Landing (¾ mile).

APPENDIX II
Accommodation, tourist and other information

For additional information see the following Tourist Information Centres:

Northumberland
see: www.visitnorthumberland.com
Bellingham TIC: The Heritage Centre, Hillside, Bellingham NE48 2GR (Tel 01434 220616)
Corbridge TIC: Hill Street, Corbridge NE45 5AA (Tel 01434 632815)
Haltwhistle TIC: Mechanics Institute, Westgate, Haltwhistle NE49 0AX (Tel 01434 322002)
Hexham TIC: Wentworth Car Park, Wentworth Place, Hexham, NE46 1QE (Tel 01434 652220)

Cumbria
see: www.visitcumbria.com
Alston TIC: Town Hall, Front Street, Alston CA9 3RF (Tel 01434 382244)

NewcastleGateshead
see: www.NewcastleGateshead.com

North Tyneside
see: www.northtynesde.gov.uk/culture_
North Shields TIC: Royal Quays, North Shields NE29 6DW (Tel 0191200 5895)

South Tyneside
see: www.visitsouthtyneside.co.uk
South Shields Visitor Information Centre: Haven Point, Pier Parade, South Shields NE33 2JS (Tel 0191 424 7788)

Further information may be available from www.daftasabrush.org.uk